A 5 YEAR PLAN TO SAVE OUR PLANET

GLOBAL RENAISSANCE

STEVEN HACKIN

PREFACE
ROBERT MULLER fmr. UN Asst. Secretary-General

GLOBE PRESS   LOS ANGELES

Published by GLOBE PRESS

Library of Congress Cataloging in Publication Data.

ISBN 1-879081-99-7

Printed in The United States of America

GF 75 .H33 1992
Hackin, Steven.
Global renaissance

DEDICATED TO

DREAMERS AND REALISTS OF ALL AGES

CONTENTS

ACKNOWLEDGMENTS

I would like to express my thanks to numerous colleagues and other concerned people who read and made suggestions as the manuscript took shape.

I owe a special debt of gratitude to Ry Hay, Dr. Alan Sager and Judge Howard Hantman for generously assisting in editing the final draft.

My deepest appreciation is extended to Dennis Hackin for ideas, support and enthusiasm during the years spent working on the book.

A great debt of thanks is owed the hundreds of researchers, journalists, scholars, environmentalists and futurist without whose works this would not have come about.

PREFACE

For more than forty years in the United Nations I have seen the birth of one global problem after the other. And while the growing threats are building up behind the backs of our leaders, they mostly go about their business as usual, hoping for the best, relishing their old beliefs and sovereignties and neglecting our planet and their best global instrument the United Nations.

Global Renaissance has two outstanding merits: it gives the most concise, impressive and thoroughly researched information on our global predicaments. I have never seen anything like it. Secondly, it gives the solution, the only solution: The Presidents of the US and Russia must urgently get together and change the course of things.

My wish, prayer and recommendation is that the book be on the night tables not only of these two leaders, but of all heads of states who run this planet, of all heads of corporations and religions, parliamentarians, governors, mayors, heads of the media, university presidents, professors of political science, teachers, journalists, students, concerned citizens and grass-root organizations.

It provides the necessary shock treatment needed to change the course of the world. It has the perfect diagnosis and it has the perfect cure. I pray God and the saints, if they love this beautiful Earth and humanity to help this message find its way and reach innumerable people and the leaders on our planet.

And thank you, Steven Hackin, for having studied and condensed the vital global information and warnings issued by the most important institution on Earth the United Nations. After all, we may not have preached in the desert for nothing during all these past forty five years.

Robert Muller
former UN Assistant Secretary-General
Chancellor of the University for Peace

INTRODUCTION

Whether the coming century will be a golden age or the last one for humankind depends upon the actions of every person on the planet. Today, humanity is no longer a clan, a city-state or a country. We are a world civilization.

By solving our common global problems the next stage in history can be a Global Renaissance. A time when society truly flowers. Where music, the arts, literature, sports, science and individual pursuits come to life. The world will be without atomic bombs. The skies and rivers on the continents will be pristine. A wonderful new culture will evolve.

With the advent of two-way television, computers and robots, workweeks will diminish to thirty hours. Around our globe people will feel a new spirit. Seemingly unachievable goals in a short period will be achieved bringing a shining sense of optimism and joy. Everywhere people will be part of a Global Renaissance—grand, majestic and mystical.

Trillions of dollars from the peace dividend as a result of disarmament will be used to sustain a prosperous global economy. By keying in on United Nations standards, the grain harvests on farms and the fish in the oceans will be plentiful with massive food reserves at the North Pole.

INTRODUCTION

Industry and offices will be pollution free. The sun will power automobiles, monorails and airplanes.

Most of the excitement and activity during the Global Renaissance will take place in the cities and towns. Modern electronic homes will go up with gardens and entertainment centers. There will be a strong sense of community and great local pride. People will be very much aware that they are living in a special and exciting age. Young and old alike will see the beauty in themselves and nature. Unlike ever before people will be free, and have leisure, education, travel and a lifespan near one hundred. In the years to come either humanity finds ways to live healthy, happy and wise around our planet, or perishes.

The Renaissance in the 1300s, 1400s and 1500s in cities and towns in Europe marked the end of the Dark Ages and the beginning of a wonderful time for many to be alive. Society went through great changes. It was a new age of thinking and learning. It was an era of astonishing inventions. Clocks became popular. Waterwheels ran factories. The printing press was developed. The discovery in astronomy that the Earth revolved around the sun was made. Daring explorers set out on uncharted seas and discovered the new world

The spirit of confidence and reason that characterized the Renaissance affected people all over. Peasants rebelled against kings. Humble priests spoke out against the wealth of Rome. People became more aware of themselves as individuals.

The enlightenment's optimism that the spread of knowledge would bring happiness to humanity inspired artists, musicians, craftsmen, scholars, architects, philosophers as well as governments. The classics were revived and civilization ripened. The Renaissance were effervescent and exciting centuries sparked with vital ideas, events, personalities and families.

GLOBAL RENAISSANCE

However, hundreds of years of tragic neglect, short sightedness and misguided policies have brought us to the point where six crisis in pollution, population, energy, food, housing and weapons threaten the destruction of the Earth. No one can escape. The Presidents of the United States and Russia and their families, like the rest of us 5 billion[1], are all in the same dangerous predicament.

52,000 nuclear weapons[2] are in arsenals with enough radioactive fallout to destroy all life on the planet twelve times.[3] The population is exploding at the rate of 250,000 babies a day.[4] The air we breathe is heavily polluted. 500 million people are chronically hungry.[5] Our food is fraught with chemicals. The petroleum supply is dangerously low. The ozone layer is being destroyed. Cancer and AIDS are spreading.

These conditions confronting our global village cannot be tackled on the basis of old ideas carried over from previous centuries. New thinking is called for. Much that was inconceivable five years ago and unlikely six months ago has somehow, against all odds come to pass. The astonishing events in Russia, the commonwealth and Eastern Europe by millions of people in nonviolent revolutions show that unprecedented change can happen in a short time.

Precisely because global solutions require difficult adjustments an immediate confidential dialogue between the superpower presidents will therefore be not only necessary but unavoidable. It's purpose must be to clarify the international goals, set the agenda by the key players and schedule a turnaround.

In a matter of a few hours or a few days, after the two statesmen talk by two-way television the 4,300 strategic nuclear launchers[6] endangering the entire planet can be shut down. After a week of historic meetings the US President and the Russian President in consultation with leaders from Europe, Japan, China and India can work out a way to divert

INTRODUCTION

more than 1 trillion dollars[7] that were to be spent on weapons into Renaissance programs.

Hundreds of millions of new jobs will open up around the globe to solve our common international problems and to advance medicine, genetics, robotics, aquafarming, geodesic construction and space exploration. The unemployment rolls will drop on all the continents. Enlightened choices will be made. A dynamic new world will develop.

The international banking community, the IMF and World Bank will roll over 2 trillion dollars of old debts to Third World and Communist countries[8], and provide technical assistance and a comprehensive package of loans and credits for long term renewal projects. The Russian Federation will become a member of the World Bank.

In the months ahead civilization can end near atomic annihilation and begin a great golden age. The best and the brightest of the first Renaissance in spirit and values can be reborn. People will get involved in issues, vote, as well as eat healthy, not pollute and recycle. Activities will flourish all over. Here will be wonderful opportunities and a new way of life. The American Renaissance, Russian Renaissance, European Renaissance, Asian Renaissance, African Renaissance and South American Renaissance will be underway. The future promises to be truly brilliant.

Today all leaders, especially in the United States, Russia and Europe, must be honest with themselves and face reality a good deal more realistically. The recent superpower summit, like other summits, talked about numerous problems but settled none. The world is not safer. The underlying problems haven't gone away. In fact each day they get more deadly and costly.

Humankind is at a crossroad. We have entered an era in which our actions and relationship to nature and technology will determine our destiny. Conditions considered politically or economically impossible can be accomplished in a remarkably brief period given the belief that survival is at stake.

The times to come are completely open to new bold step by step decisions. However, in the next five years if the needed city, national and global reforms are delayed conditions will dramatically worsen for everyone.

Clearly, the world has an interest in solving the impending catastrophe. What lies ahead, or what can lie ahead if the efforts are pursued is what this book is about.

A great effort was made to utilize the best scientific research, supplemented with the latest data from governments, the UN and future institutes. The world computer models were chosen to provide a quantitative basis for the projections. Hopefully, the knowledge will be useful and broaden our understanding of how we respond to today's world.

CHAPTER 1

THE FUTURE OF WAR
OR PEACE

Around the globe there is a general consensus that nuclear and conventional weapons have eclipsed all other international problems. The trillion dollars spent on arms makes munitions one of the largest industries in the world. Weapons procurement has created powerful multinational corporations with interlocking directorates that dominate the global economy. It fosters politicians and bureaucracies orientated to staying in power through further arms expenditures.

This week Democratic, Socialist and Communist governments are under pressure to support military industries by maximizing sales in various ways to Third World or other nations. However, the superpowers will give away vis-a-vis grants, aid, or surplus more weapons and military equipment than they will make in direct sales. Developing countries have increased their arms budgets fivefold in the past two decades. Some are spending more on their military than on education, health, welfare and the environment.

In the 1970s, 80s and 90s military expenditures purchased massive quantities of armaments which are deployed or stockpiled in depots and armories (Chart 1). Countries on all the continents are importing weapons, precision-guided missiles, new tanks, anti-satellites and stealth

GLOBAL RENAISSANCE

CHART 1

WORLD MILITARY
EXPENDITURES

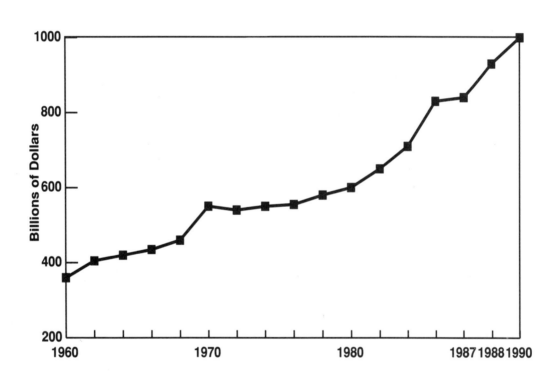

Source: "World Military and Social Expenditures," 1991

fighters, even when they fulfill no real need (Chart 2).

The arms build up raises the opportunity for escalation from conventional to nuclear war via a miscalculation, accident or unauthorized use; and increases the dangers of every regional conflict, particularly in the Middle East, erupting into World War III.

At 13 nuclear weapons facilities including Savannah River, Idaho, Pantex, Hanford, Rocky Flats and Oak Ridge 82,320 people are producing atomic weapons.[1] In Russia and the commonwealth similar plants and personnel are involved in nuclear production. Between 5 and 10 million people are directly engaged in defense work. There are 150 major plants to assemble the military machinery and warheads.[2]

If trends continue over the course of the next year 2,920 nuclear missiles will be shipped to depots. 1,557 fighter and bomber aircraft can be expected in the skies. 30 new Navy warships will be launched and at sea.[3] Obviously, the balance of terror doesn't serve anybodies interest. The planet is too small and the weapons too destructive for more wars. No one can any longer have the illusion that there won't be a nuclear catastrophe if the nukes remain up.

However, there was a time when there weren't any weapons anywhere on the Earth. In fact, until 1945, not a single atomic bomb or nuclear missile had been built or detonated. Then in August the skies over Japan light up for miles. The first atomic bomb explodes. Within seconds Hiroshima was engulfed in radiation and fire. 271,000 people were dying.[4]

The US had 3 nuclear weapons in 1946. Russia and the former USSR exploded its first Atomic bomb in 1949 and began deployment in 1956. By 1958 the superpowers had intercontinental ballistic missiles. In ten years multiple warheads existed in both arsenals.[5] The point was reached when the world could be destroyed from nuclear annihilation.

CHART 2

WORLD ARMS IMPORTS

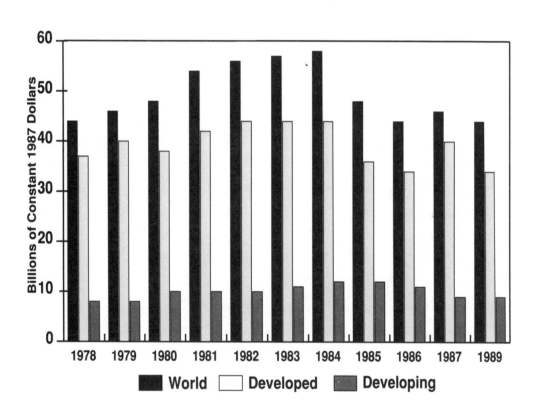

Source: "World Military Expenditures and Arms Transfers," 1990

American and Soviet diplomats realized the ultimate dangers and offered proposals for destroying all weapons, however discussions stalled.

The 1970s, 80s and 90s witnessed the US and Russia/CIS blindly hasten the development of more accurate and destructive weaponry (Chart 3). During the last decade, 7 trillion dollars were spent on the military.[6] Around the globe some 50 per cent of the skilled scientific manpower is engaged in military research and development.[7]

Currently, six nations build nuclear weapons, United States, Russia, Great Britain, France, China and India. As trends are moving, unless international actions are taken 48 countries that have nuclear reactors could make atomic bombs from spent plutonium rods.[8]

The US ICBM force, thousands of missiles, stand posed to attack the Russian heartland. They have a combined firepower of over 100,000 Hiroshima explosions. The Russians have a similar stockpile of missiles aimed at America. One US Polaris submarine can simultaneously attack Moscow, St. Petersburg, Kiev, Tashkent, Baku, Kharkov, Gorky, Novosibirsk, Kuibyshev, and Sverdlovsk. These ten cities, each with a population of over one million, would be immediately destroyed. The United States has over 30 such submarines.[9]

Some 25 per cent of the American people are concentrated in ten metropolitan areas, so the Russians can paralyze these urban centers using only a small part of their firepower. However, if bombed all organized life in the US will end. The Russian Typhoon submarine is equipped with 20 long-range ballistic missiles, each armed with 12 warheads. Over 200 US cities can be struck by one Typhoon sub.[10]

The result is a hair trigger situation in which either the US President or the Russian President have very little time to make the appropriate decision, perhaps minutes in an attack or what is falsely perceived to be an attack. There is no recall once the command is given.

GLOBAL RENAISSANCE

CHART 3

US AND RUSSIAN/CIS
NUCLEAR ARSENAL

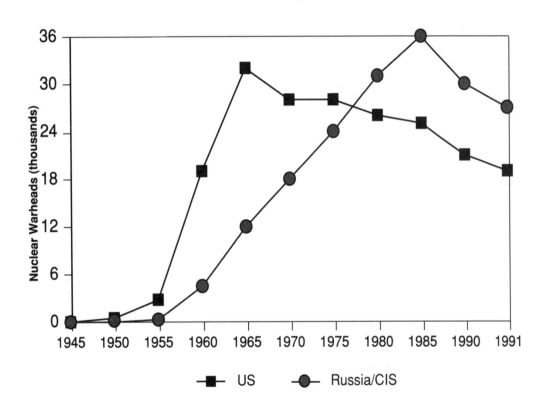

Source: The Bulletin of the Atomic Scientists
Nuclear Weapons Databook

THE FUTURE OF WAR OR PEACE

That means that if the nuclear button is ever pressed, we are irrevocably committed to a nuclear war.[11]

In the first World War, 1914-1918, in which horses and 70 mile cannons were used, chemical weapons did extensive damage and killed hundreds of thousands of people. After the war widespread public condemnation, led to the Geneva Protocol of 1925 which prohibits the use of chemical and biological weapons.[12]

However, the Russians, who suffered terrible from chemical weapons developed a large array of munitions filled with lethal compounds. The United States followed with a considerable chemical stockpile. The nerve agents that make up most of the chemical arsenal are quite similar to pesticides. It is possible to turn a pesticide factory into a weapons facility by altering a few chemical processes.[13]

16 nations already have chemical war capabilities and six others are acquiring them. Iraq is known to have used chemical weapons in its war with Iran killing thousands. The current Russian and commonwealth stockpile of chemical and biological weapons is about 350,000 tons of lethal agents. The US chemical stockpile probably is smaller. There are about 8,000 tons of nerve agent, available in bombs and shells. A larger amount of lethal compounds is stored.[14]

Biological warfare and modern chemical weapons are capable of rendering battlefields and vast surrounding areas almost unimaginably deadly for both soldiers and civilians.[15] The dangerous spread of chemical weapons and rapid deterioration of respect for existing international norms call for urgent action.[16]

In outer space the Russian Federation and the USA are conducting an arms race. The communications, navigation, early warning, and anti-satellites are now used by both sides. If laser weapons, designed to destroy targets on Earth or space, are put into orbit, the problem will be extended. This danger exists.[17]

The US and Russian plans for space militarization will not enhance the security of either country. For each will not stand quietly watching. Appropriate counters will be developed and the arms race will escalate.

Arms sales raise the industrial production and provide a means for balancing national and international accounts. However, the airlifting by Russian and US jet transports of more dangerous conventional weapons into Central America, Africa and Asia will only continue to aggravate the poverty and social unrest. The evident strain on the global economy is widespread. Military spending contributes to inflation, raises unemployment and diverts resources urgently needed for economic development. National and international security is not enhanced but seriously undermined.

The simple truth is that the military-nuclear complex is unmanageable, obsolete and dangerous to everyone. Building more conventional and nuclear weapons in a handful of factories by a small number of people won't stop the deterioration of the conditions which all of us are struggling with.

However, cutting military spending by the superpowers, allies and 100 other nations around the globe will consequently funnel new funds into renewal projects. In the face of weak economies, socially explosive conditions and a faltering future the weapons build up has an alarming air of unreality. The arms and strategies elaborated by governments for defense are largely irrelevant to the underlying dangers and instabilities, especially with nuclear overkill.

However, the US, Russia and the commonwealth together account for 61 per cent of the world's military expenditures.[18] The superpowers and allies make up 88 per cent of total arms exports.[19] The Presidents of the US and Russia control 97 per cent of all atomic bombs.[20] A nuclear war can be launched on the decision of one of these men or accidentally by others and snuff out a massive number of lives.

Clearly, we are in an unnecessary situation where any day or any hour news may be received of US and Russian missiles firing on each other in Europe, the Middle East, Korea, Russia or America. If this occurs the superpower presidents and their top advisers will be aboard jet planes as a nuclear red alert kicks in around the world.

If New York City, Chicago, Detroit, Dallas and Los Angeles are bombed with nuclear missiles, fifty million men, women and children will die. The surrounding suburbs and rolling hills will be burning. If cruise missiles explode in St. Petersburg, Kiev, Gorky and Kharkov, these great cities and for fifty miles will be smoldering and in ruins. Sixty million Russians will be dead. If Stealth Fighters drop more bombs, mushroom clouds will rise from the decimated cities in Europe, the Americas, Africa and Asia. By then in the presidential jets the TV screens will show the superpower presidents give the historic orders to shut down all the nuclear weapons.

In ten minutes 481 US and Russian/CIS strategic long range bombers carrying atomic bombs will be grounded or turned back to bases. In fifteen minutes 2,408 land based intercontinental ballistic missiles in North America and Europe will be shut off.[21] By twenty minutes, 452 submarines equipped with nukes on patrol in the Pacific, Atlantic and Indian Oceans will switch off the last of the atomic weapons.[22]

However, the direct effects of a nuclear exchange will kill hundreds of millions. The radius of the explosion will remain contaminated for thousands of years. The indirect effects will kill billions.[23] The breakdown of transportation, hospital and other systems will compound the difficulties caused by starvation, water and energy shortages. The clouds of smoke will reduce sunlight, alter weather and influence climate. A massive depletion of ozone will result. In a matter of months radiation will kill 5 billion humans and all the myriad of life leaving a wasteland planet.

Today with mass communication there is a global consciousness that transcends national boundaries, old animosities and outdated ideas. Military, industrial, agricultural and economic strength predestines America and Russia to take the lead. The President of the US and the President of Russia through the close coordination of disarmament, monetary and trade policies can in a short period of time adjust the global economy to the new realities.

The superpowers along with their allies can divert more than 1 trillion dollars scheduled for the military through their ministries into development programs in housing, education, the arts, health, pollution control and farming. Studies have shown that military expenditures create only half as many jobs as in basic industries.[24]

The income of 2.6 billion people in the 44 poorest countries can double. The fuel consumed by the Pentagon in a single year would run the entire US public transit system for 22 years.[25] Installation in the Third World of 300,000 hand pumps to give villages access to safe water would be the cost of 2 fighter aircraft. The operating expense of an antisubmarine cruiser would house three-fourths of the homeless families in London. Discontinuing the research on Star Wars would provide an elementary education for 1.4 million children in Latin America. A campaign for global eradication of smallpox would be the cost of 2 navy frigates and create annual savings 10 times the investment.[26]

Phasing out the Stealth bomber program would provide 79 billion dollars most of the costs to meet US clean water goals by 2000.[27]   50 billion dollars in military outlays reappropriated could double public expenditures of the health care of 4 billion people in the Third World, providing immunization to every baby and fresh water and basic sanitation within 10 years to every village.[28]

Russia by reallocating the military budget can double education and health care. In the United States, Europe and other countries the per capita expenditures transferred from the armed services to public services can increase dramatically.[29]

If the US President, the Russian President and their ruling councils adjust policies then the budgets for economic assistance to the poorer countries will increase substantially. Hydroelectric generators, medical clinics, battery tractors and solar autos can be imported into Third World Democratic market societies. The GNP for the developed and developing countries will rise, jobs increase and life improve significantly. However, if military growth continues at the same rate in the production and stockpile of missiles, weapons, tanks, ships, ammunition and bases, by the year 2000 national governments will spend an additional 10 trillion dollars.[30]

Right now, the US President and the Russian President can initiate a course of events moving from mutual disarmament into a Global Renaissance. When international military expenditures are discontinued, deficits and taxes can drop considerably. Surplus revenues can be made available for an array of renewal projects. Models and prototypes with able staffs are currently operating in all countries.

Prime ministers and congresses in Europe, India and China can join in the talks, work out the details, unravel the problems, and find solutions in a cooperative and constructive fashion. At United Nations headquarters in New York the Secretary-General and diplomats from Security Council countries can arrange and coordinate the time sched-

GLOBAL RENAISSANCE

ules.

At televised ceremonies from Washington and Moscow the US President and the Russian President can historically inaugurate a Global Renaissance. Hundreds of millions of Americans will turn out coast to coast at festivals, rock concerts and family get togethers. Russians will fill Red Square and parks with singing and dancing. The dual tracks of mutual disarmament and world development will be underway in Europe, Asia, Africa and South America amidst great celebrations.

The gates at Army, Air Force and Navy bases and missile sites can be pulled open to the cheers of citizens everywhere. The first trucks carrying atomic bombs and nuclear missiles can be on the road. Cargo planes, and jumbo jets will be loaded at military airports with ammunition, jeeps and artillery guns. Military facilities will be turned into modern civic centers, universities, hospitals and health spas. 75,000 tanks[31] in Western and Eastern Europe will wind their way in jubilant parades through the cities and countryside lined with happy flag waving Europeans.

The factories in which the world's armaments are produced are the best equipped to handle the disassembly with specialized machinery and the highly skilled personnel, executives and board chairmen. The assembly lines can be reworked and within weeks the nuclear launchers and conventional weapons will begin to be dismantled. The parts, particularly from computers, high technology and medical equipment, will be transferred and used. Old smelters can reopen and unemployed men and women be hired to melt down the weapons.

Chemical weapons factories can recycle the toxins into biodegradable compounds. The existing military installations for biological warfare in the US, Russia and other countries can be converted to environmental microbiology, crop productivity, purification of sewage for drinking water, mass vaccination and problems of carcinogenesis.[32] The US and Russian Star Wars programs will be eliminated and the space technology transferred to useful fields.

The 28 million troops[33] will be reassigned to peacetime projects. In shipyards in St. Petersburg, Gdansk and Los Angeles workers can be on the decks with torches and wrenches removing the missiles and torpedoes from 129 destroyers, 20 aircraft carriers and 282 frigates.[34] In the engine rooms engineers would replace nuclear, coal and diesel engines with new motors that run on renewable energy. Around the clock war vessels would be reconditioned and converted, into hospital ships, ocean freighters, and passenger liners. This could boost tourism around the planet from about 350 million[35] to 700 million people in five years.

Today, what is required to survive is mutual and complete global arms reduction in all nations, according to a specific timetable to a minimal level consistent with the need for police to maintain domestic peace. In many ways the United States and Russia and opposing countries are almost mirror images of the others armies, tanks, missiles, navy and jets.

The superpowers and national rivals are influenced by their perception of the others' weapons and intentions, as well as their own self interests, fears and competition. Although steps toward a disarmed world may appear to be politically easier to take than a large one, almost continuous rounds of arms talks since World War II have seen the acquisition of more deadly weapons in national arsenals.

When Soviet President Gorbachev and US President Reagan signed the Intermediate Range Nuclear Force (INF) Treaty in 1987, it signaled to the world an effort toward peaceful co-existence between the superpowers. However, during the six months to Congress's ratification, both sides built more nuclear weapons than will be destroyed in the three years stipulated in the document.[36]

A two stage plan where 50 per cent of the weapons are taken down possibly looks favorable. But there is no guarantee after years of negotiations that the second crucial stage will actually get started.

The SALT I Treaty was ratified by both the US and former USSR. This accord has not limited refinements in weapons, number of atomic bombs, or the military expenditures for conventional armaments. In fact, since the signing the Russian and former Soviet forces have grown by 8,600 warheads[37] and the Americans similarly.

In 1990 lead by Presidents Gorbachev and Bush, the US, USSR and 20 allies signed the Conventional Forces Treaty in Europe (CFE). Each side would take down large numbers of weapons. However, both would keep 50,000 battle tanks and armored vehicles, 6,800 combat jets, 2,000 attack helicopters and 20,000 artillery guns. The military production lines would continue to manufacture weapons and bombs. Manpower limits would not be imposed on any armies or any cuts made. The treaty was ratified by the US Senate. Once Russia/CIS agree the reduction will take 40 months.[38]

In Moscow in August 1991 the START Treaty was signed by Presidents Bush and Gorbachev. The superpowers would each give up substantial nuclear weapons. However, both sides would retain 1,600 strategic intercontinental ballistic missiles, long range bombers, submarine launched missiles and 4,900 nuclear warheads. Atomic bombs would not have to be destroyed, only stored. Bombers and nuclear weapons could increase. Once the treaty is ratified by the US and Russia/CIS, it would take seven years to reach reductions.[39]

Even when these treaties are passed and the armaments are taken down massive numbers of troops will remain deployed with tens of thousands of tanks, jets and ships equipped with deadly conventional weapons. Worldwide major cities will still be targeted with nuclear missiles.

In September 1991 President Bush ordered 700 warheads on short range missiles in Europe and 1,000 nuclear artillery shells on longer-range missiles destroyed. The nuclear tipped Tomahawk and other tactical missiles on warships and submarines would be removed. Strategic bombers and 1,800 longe-range missile warheads were ordered off of alert. Half of the 10,000 warheads affected would be placed in storage. However, defense funds were not freed for domestic programs. Some steps would even cost money. The plan called for negotiations whereby each country limited its strategic weapons to one single warhead missile.[40]

In October 1991 President Gorbachev matched the US moves and pledged unilaterally to eliminate an additional 1,000 Soviet strategic warheads within seven years. His proposal would reduce strategic weapons by about half.[41] A few weeks later NATO decided to eliminate 3,500 nuclear weapons leaving 700 air delivered atomic bombs in Europe. The withdrawal of the atomic weapons will take two to three years.[42]

However, these superpower steps leave intact thousands of nuclear weapons ready to fire on land, in the air and at sea. In minutes the American and Russian strategic nuclear bombers and ICBM's can be put back on alert. The thousands of stored missiles can be redeployed. Even if 50 per cent of all nuclear weapons were eliminated, there still will remain enough to destroy the planet six times. Clearly, these unwise approaches will not reduce mutual global destruction.

At this moment a small per cent of the US and Russian nuclear weapons have explosives insensitive to crash or fire. There is the real risk of accidental or deliberate unauthorized launches and rogue nukes.

GLOBAL RENAISSANCE

Today, each side is locked in an old pattern striving to offset the others seeming gains by improving accuracy and building more explosive warheads, midgetman missiles, mobile launchers and space lasers.

There is the possibility with a change in leaders that a superpower or other war may break out. If one side is losing conventionally with tanks and artillery, someone might decide to use nuclear weapons. Nobody really knows with confidence how World War III would end.

Projections indicate that the military systems could be dismantled, transported back to the factories and disassembled in 5 years. Rapid verifiable disarmament would eliminate any chance of an eventual war ever starting, and assure a stable, sustained and peaceful future.

In the long run, or even in the next 24 hours, where does the weapons spiral get us? Why should we continue with the shadow of the H-Bomb hanging over our heads? Do we need to suffer a war or do the Russians or the world?

The START Treaty, INF, CFE and the Chemical Weapons talks provide the framework for disarmament. A reduction down to zero is the basis for the best agreement and the only one that will work. Daily monitoring via reconnaissance satellites and on site inspection will verify the results. Simultaneously, while this is happening the Renaissance will be underway locally, nationally and globally. It is not too late for the White House and Moscow to prevent a nuclear holocaust. There is a new basis of settlement and the means to work realistically together. Leaders worldwide can abandon the dead end courses and transform history in the years to come.

Public opinion in major cities indicate very few if any people are for a nuclear war, most prefer mutual disarmament and international development. However, today the arms talks between the United States and Russia are at a standstill. Forty years of negotiations for partial measures offers little hope that the next rounds will achieve a reversal of the increase in weapons.

All countries are inclined to give up the high expenditures for armaments permanently in favor of an equitable peace time economy, as long as the US and Russia provide the global leadership. The chances are favorable for Washington and Moscow to alter today's military circumstances and bring on a condition of economic and ecological stability that is sustainable far into the future.

Mutual disarmament and a Global Renaissance are compatible with the interests of people in all nations, despite differences in ideology and standard of living. The renewal programs undoubtedly will differ. But there would be massive international demands for consumer goods, industrial machinery, food and technology. In turn, this would lead to expanded domestic production and an upswing in national economies.

Given the nature of present day weapons, no country can have any hope of safeguarding itself with military means. Security can only be mutual. Nearly everybody agrees that someday all the nuclear weapons have to be dismantled. For the first time in years arms control experts are voicing hope that an effective international agreement can be worked out to rid the planet of weapons. Not long ago a disengagement of the Warsaw Pact forces in Europe seemed inconceivable. Now it is reality. With the changes in Russia, Germany, Poland, Czechoslovakia, Hungry, Romania, Bulgaria, Albania, and other nations, massive worldwide disarmament seems possible, even likely.

The superpower presidents have a global responsibility which transcends all others. Today, the whole situation can be turned around with a telephone call and some realistic international approaches. Then there will be every reason to believe in one, five or ten years from now that living conditions in general will not be dangerous but prosperous.

CHAPTER 2

AIR, LAND AND WATER
TODAY AND TOMORROW

The planet is teeming with life. The tropics, forests and deserts in the Americas, Africa, Asia and Europe abound with animals and plants. A myriad of fish and flora inhabit the rivers and oceans. In the skies flocks of birds are seen flying on their seasonal migrations. In many regards we are living in a paradise. Of the planets in the solar system only the Earth has the miracle of life.

However, pollution in the air, land and water has reached a point where the global environment is at a crisis stage. American astronauts and Russian cosmonauts in their transmissions from the US shuttle and the Mir space station have noted the dark smog over the cities.

Nearly all of the scientific studies in the international community are in general agreement on the danger of the problems, the sources, and the threat posed to our common future. Rising levels of toxic chemicals, sewage, automobile exhaust, aerosols in the atmosphere, heavy metals, water pollutants and nuclear waste are documented locally and nationally which show the magnitude of the build up (Chart 4, Chart 5).

The United States is the predominant industrial power and accordingly megapolluter. The air emissions of pollutants into the atmosphere as a result of human activities amount to about 609 million tons of

AIR, LAND AND WATER - TODAY AND TOMORROW

CHART 4

**AIR QUALITY ABOVE
NATIONAL STANDARDS**

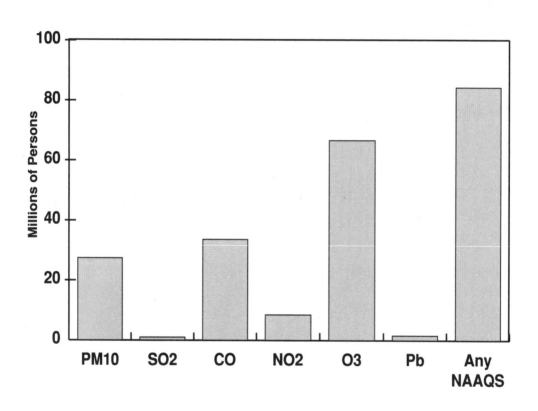

*Source: US Environmental Protection Agency
National Air Quality and Emissions Trend Report*

CHART 5

NUCLEAR WASTES

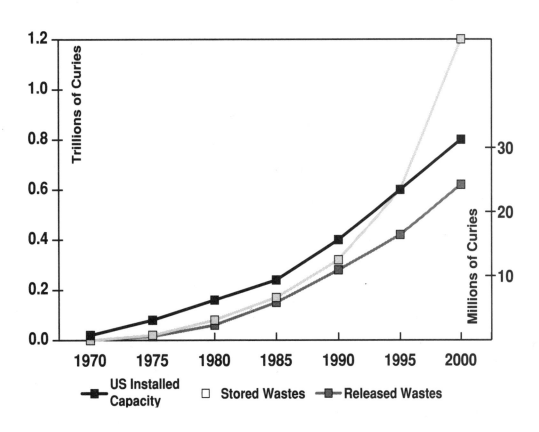

Source: Nuclear Regulatory Commission

AIR, LAND AND WATER - TODAY AND TOMORROW

Carbon Monoxide, 211 million tons of Sulphur Oxide, 185 million tons of Organic Compounds, 199 million tons of Nitrogen Oxide, 72 million tons of lead and 59 million tons of particulates.[1] Europe adds approximately 2 billion tons of pollution. Including Russia, China and India the world generates 13 billion tons.[2]

The global factories, transport system, network of cities and hundreds of millions of vehicles, require energy to operate. Currently the world is burning massive quantities of nonrenewable fuel from petroleum and coal. This is the primary source of air pollution. In the United States 39 per cent is generated from autos, trains and planes, 36 per cent from utilities and fuel combustion and 25 per cent from industry.[3]

Between 1900 and today, lead concentrations from industrialization in Greenland snow have increased 16 fold (Chart 6). Air pollution has adverse effects on human health, agriculture, forests, animals, wateresources and the deterioration of buildings worldwide. Some 990 million people in London, Rome, Madrid and other cities are exposed to unhealthy levels of sulphur dioxide in the air. 1 billion people living in New York, Houston, Toronto, Osaka and other urban areas are breathing excessive levels of suspended particulates.[4] Air pollution related health problems now span all the continents. In Athens, Greece the number of deaths rises six fold on heavily polluted days. In Hungry every seventeenth death is caused by air pollution.[5]

Across Europe 124 million acres of forests 35 per cent of the total trees have been damaged by the continued effects of acid rains.[6] Acidic deposition has effected the water in Scandinavia where major fish populations in thousands of lakes have died. In Canada 150,000 lakes suffer some biological damage from acid rain. While the United States has about 1,000 acidified lakes.[7]

GLOBAL RENAISSANCE

CHART 6

LEAD IN THE GREENLAND
ICE CAP

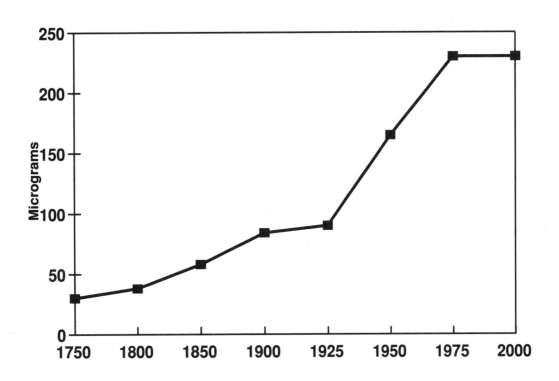

Source: "Lead in the Modern Environment—How much is Natural?"
CC Patterson and JD Salvia

AIR, LAND AND WATER - TODAY AND TOMORROW

The European rivers have the highest average levels of Ammonia 14 times and nitrates 45 times above natural levels in unpolluted rivers.[8] Acidification of ground water supples has been reported from North America to Sweden. In some areas the concentration of copper, zinc, cadmium and aluminium are often 10 to 100 times larger than in neutral ground water. The presence of these metals in drinking water can result in a number of serious human health problems.[9]

In India 70 per cent of the surface water is polluted. China's rivers suffer from increasing pollution loads due to untreated sewage and industrial waste. 40 major rivers in Malaysia are so polluted that they are nearly devoid of fish and aquatic mammals, the main pollutants being rubber processing residues, sewage, and wastes from factories.[10]

Industries across the United States generate 7.6 billion tons of solid waste per year. Oil and gas produces 2 to 3 billion tons, mining operations about 1.4 billion tons. The vast majority of the waste facilities are unlined impoundments.[11] In the US there are 76,000 active industrial landfills from which contaminants may leach to ground water. Thousands of underground steel storage tanks for petroleum products are not protected against corrosion. Chemical contamination of ground water has already closed more than 1,100 wells and there are about 7,700 sites where ground water has been fouled to varying degrees. Unhealthy water resulting from the field application of pesticides had been confirmed in California, New York and Florida.[12]

American municipal waste production has grown to 158 million tons, enough to fill a convoy of garbage trucks, 145,000 miles long, 6 times around the Earth. Only 25 percent of city landfills monitor groundwater for possible pollution. Less than 16 percent have liners. Only 5 percent collect the polluted liquid waste. These practices suggest that a large portion of landfilled municipal solid waste ends up in places where it might contaminate ground water.[13] Similar environmental conditions exist in Russia, Eastern Europe, Japan and worldwide.

Contaminations by industrial chemicals in communities as Love Canal in the US and Seveso in Italy have led to permanent evacuations. In Brazil, where concentrations of industrial wastes along the southern coast have reached life threatening levels, the city of Cubatao is locally referred to as the Valley of Death.[14] In some cities chemical and nuclear accidents have reached epidemic proportions, Bhopal in India, and the Ukraine's Cherynoble where hundreds of thousands of people had to be evacuated. The medical results are high rates of Leukemia, heart disease, lung problems and death. The cost is hundreds of billions of dollars.

Toxic and hazardous waste are a by product of unregulated global industrial activity. 420 million tons a year are produced. It contaminates whatever environment, air, sea or soil it enters.[15] In the US of the 1,219 declared hazardous waste sites only a few have been cleaned up (Chart 7). Industrialized countries are in comparable situations. In the Atlantic Ocean during a fifteen year period the European countries dumped 94,000 tons of nuclear waste. The radioactivity went from 250 curies to 1428 and the beta-gamma activity from 7,600 to 50,000 curies.[16]

The loss of forest and species is not only a national disaster, but the future of all of humanity is affected. Tropical rain forests protect watersheds for farmers who grow food for over 1 billion people. They are important regulators of world climate, provide valuable timber and fuel wood, harbor irreplaceable genetic resources and generate vital quantities of oxygen to breath.[17] Between 35 and 50 million acres of tropical forest are lost every year. Of the Earth's total biological diversity 25 per cent is at serious risk of extinction during the next 20 to 30 years.[18]

During the past two decades the poorer countries of the develop-

AIR, LAND AND WATER - TODAY AND TOMORROW

CHART 7

HAZARDOUS SITES

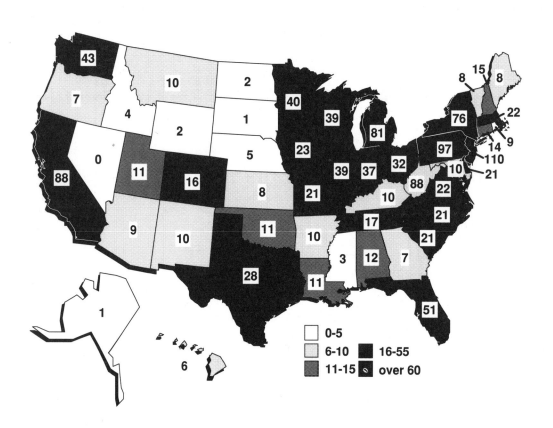

Total Sites in US: 1,219

Source: US Environmental Protection Agency
National Priorities List Fact Book

ing world have experienced a massive depletion of forests, soils, fisheries, waters, the atmosphere and species. Just 40 years ago Ethiopia had a 30 per cent forest cover and today it may be 1 per cent. Until this century, India's forest covered more than half of the country. Today they are down to 14 per cent. In Africa 29 trees are being cut for every one planted. Forest areas nearly equal to the size of Britain are disappearing every year.[19]

An area larger than the African continent and inhabited by more than one billion people is now at risk from desertification. 15 million acres will turn to desert this year. Top soil loss will be roughly 25 billion tons the amount that covers Australia's wheatlands. Water use has doubled at least twice in this century and could double again over the next two decades. However, in 80 developing countries having 40 per cent of the world's population, water is already a serious constraint on development.[20]

It has become increasingly difficult to keep our freshwater supplies free of dangerous contaminants. In developing nations the greatest fouler of fresh water is sewage. The waterborne diseases spawned by biological pollution cause 80 per cent of all child deaths in the Third World. In Asian cities sanitation systems can't cope with soaring populations. Cairo's sewage floods the streets. The river which passes by New Delhi, India picks up 50 million gallons of untreated waste water every day and delivers this sludge to the unfortunate people living down river.[21]

Because sanitation systems are more sophisticated in the United States, Russia, Europe and Japan water polluted by waste is less of a health issue. However, much of the water supply has become tainted by a growing number of toxic chemicals. More than 700 have been detected in US drinking water, 129 of which the EPA calls dangerous. Poisonous industrial solvents and metals were spewed illegally into waterways and waste treatment facilities by manufacturers. 627 industrial plants and 12 federal installations dumped toxic substances into the nations waters this year.[22]

US industry releases annually about 10 billion pounds of toxics into streams and rivers. The Rocky Flats nuclear weapons plant in Colorado is accused of having discharged hazardous chemicals and radioactive contaminants into creeks leading to Denver's drinking water supplies. In 49 out of 50 states there is chemically polluted surface water. The underground water reserves which provide 60 per cent of the American population with drinking water, have become contaminated by seepage from underground chemical storage tanks and toxic leakage from landfills. In cities across America waterworks do not filter out these hazardous chemicals. Treatment plants currently aren't equipped to test and filter these toxics from our drinking water. The results are that the arsenic, barium, cadmium, mercury and a host of other pollutants are responsible for health problems ranging from stomach disorders and insomnia to liver and kidney dysfunction, cancer and birth defects.[23] Due to the intense use of toxics in the US the rate of cancer is rising by 2 per cent each year.[24] Russia, Japan and all other industrialized countries have similar conditions.

Nearly every day the news is filled with an oil spill somewhere around the world, California or New York beaches, Alaska, Canada, Europe, the Mediterranean, Japan, the Persian Gulf and Antarctic. Millions of barrels of oil leaks out from ships and barges into the oceans and waterways. Some nearby cities have had to declare disaster emergencies due to contaminated drinking water. The clean up efforts take years and are costly. The ecosystems and Salmon and Herring fishing have been destroyed. Tens of thousands of birds and sea animals have been killed.

GLOBAL RENAISSANCE

Although pollution of rivers and lakes is potentially reversible, that is not the case for groundwater. In Europe and the US where groundwater represents a significant source of fresh water, between 5 and 10 per cent of all wells examined are found to have nitrate levels higher than the maximum recommended value. Because groundwater is cut off from the atmosphere's oxygen supply, its capacity for self-purification is very low. The microbes that normally break down organic pollutants need oxygen to do their job. Prevention of contamination is the only rational approach.[25]

The future of the human species and many others are being compromised unless there is significant improvement in the management of water, waste and resources. Around the Earth species in danger of becoming extinct throughout all or a significant part of their natural range number 290 mammals, 221 birds, 74 reptiles, 13 amphibians, 58 fish and 215 invertebrates and plants.[26] Within each species there are millions of living creatures. Many of which are dying needlessly. While no reasonable individual intends to destroy the source of food, the water and the environment, in the last fifty years collectively billions of people have greatly endangered the natural systems of which all of us depend to survive.

The high levels of food production which sustains people living in Washington, Moscow, Peking, New Delhi and globally are made possible by the output of tremendous amounts of petrol-fertilizers and pesticides. Today the growth in cities and the population explosion are pouring out huge concentrations of industrial waste and sewage which is passed into the nearest river or lake, often without treatment. The effluent eventually flows to the oceans. Many toxic substances concentrate in food chains. As materials pass from plants to fish to man, the dangers to human health increase. The pollutants are reaching the upper atmosphere and the depths of the oceans. People are moving into the tropics and deserts in increasing numbers and polluting these areas.

The US President, the Russian President and most government leaders in attempting to handle the crisis are moving dangerously slow. And, contrary to what nearly all public officials are saying, the environment is not getting better. In fact, except in a few cities, the biosphere is seriously deteriorating. During the last five years the clean air and water standards in major metropolitan centers, rather than being raised have been dramatically lowered.

The ozone layer 9 to 12 miles above the earth which shields the dangerous ultraviolet rays has major holes in it the result of chlorofluorocarbons used in refrigeration and other emissions. This has upset the radiation balance and will lead to serious health hazards, as well as the destruction of plant and animal species, including marine life.[27] The Arctic ozone hole is the size of Greenland. Projections indicate a 10 per cent depletion of the ozone layer around the Earth by the year 2050. This dramatic reduction in ozone protection will result in 2 million additional skin cancer cases annually. The human immune system will make people more vulnerable to a host of infectious diseases.[28] The increase in UV-B radiation will lead to 100,000 blind persons all over the planet.[29] The health and safety of billions of people are at stake.

If the Greenhouse Effect continues with the emission at current rates of gases like carbon dioxide their concentration in the atmosphere will be equivalent to a doubling of preindustrial levels by the early part of the next century.[30] (Chart 8) This will likely result in a global temperature rise of between 1 degree C by the year 2020 and 3 degrees C before the end of next century, an increase with serious implications for all life on Earth. The most significant impacts will be a rise in sea level and radical shifts in crop patterns.[31]

CHART 8

GLOBAL TEMPERATURE
INCREASES

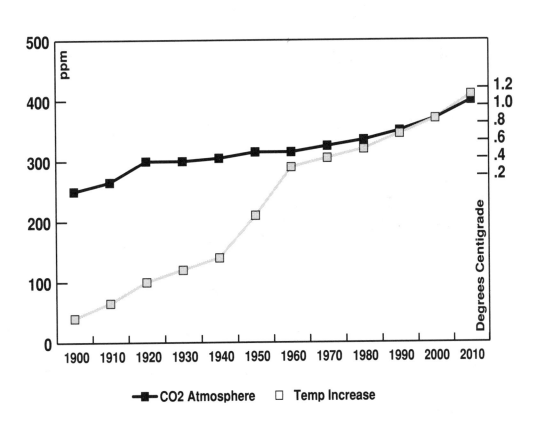

Source: United Nations Environment Programme

AIR, LAND AND WATER - TODAY AND TOMORROW

The industrial revolution began in the 1700s with the advent of machines, a petroleum economy and mass production. In the 1900s some two hundred years later the overloading of the biosphere with thousands of pollutants, and hundreds of billions of tons, combined with the uncontrollable compounding effect of toxic chemicals has produced a sudden dangerous collapse in the global environment.

If more unexpected holes appear in the ozone layer and the temperature rises at accelerated record rates floods will ensue in Los Angeles, Moscow, Amsterdam, Tokyo and coastal cities. Spontaneous explosions at hazardous waste sites, chemical plants, nuclear reactors and weapons factories in Russia, the US, Japan, India and China will occur.

If the superpower presidents, the UN Secretary General and others let the environment dangerously deteriorate to the point of no return. Then Cancer, Tuberculosis and infectious diseases will rise at alarming rates. Hospitals, schools and day care centers would find millions dying. Chaos and suffering would be widespread. Plankton in the oceans could not survive forcing a massive loss of the marine life. Crops will be massively destroyed. The death toll on the continents will dramatically rise into the billions.

Then the US and Russian leaders will be forced to send supersonic jets with scientists to the ozone holes to determine how the disintegration can be controlled and stopped. An attempt will be made to devise a strategy to save the ozone and the environment. Government officials, the police, military and doctors will be mobilized into emergency action. But in a matter of months the death toll could rise past four billion. The food and water will become contaminated. Airborne plagues could spread across the continents. Those in power would desperately try to outlast the cataclysm in shelters. Great cities will become deserted in shrouds of smog. Ten thousand years of civilization could be near extinction. The last of the humans wearing gas masks, eventually would choke to death on the petrol-nuclear air.

If changes aren't made in the global environment then the 21st century is going to be a disaster. Given the urgency, scale and widespread crisis, the efforts currently underway in Washington, Moscow and elsewhere to clean up the pollution falls far short of what is needed for survival. All over our global village everyone is affected, and will continue to be until the biosphere is brought back to life.

Today in Moscow the Russian President could be in a video-conference room looking up at the screen at the US President in the White House. The statesmen could be working out the details to a long range international plan to preserve the planet. Advisers, cabinet members, decision makers, development planners and scientists can provide counsel. The commander-in-chiefs using connected computers can determine the problems, solutions and costs, and coordinate with world leaders a series of monumental actions.

The expenditures to clean up the global environment are astronomical. 4 per cent of GNP would amount to 800 billion dollars.[32] 10 billion for West Germany, 1.5 billion for the Netherlands and 60 million for Denmark for hazardous waste.[33] 6 nations of Eastern Europe face an ecological disaster that will cost 200 billion dollars.[34] Developing countries cannot afford financial burdens on this scale, but neither can they afford the cost to their people and the world's environment. To implement the US Clean Air Act Amendments of 1990 for the government and private sector the operating expenses, interest and depreciation will amount to 120 billion annually.[35] New capital investments in manufacturing sectors of the economy for equipment are 9 billion dollars.[36] The clean up costs required to reduce the dangers of radioactive emissions are 150 billion dollars.[37]

The economic activity in each country must account for the environmental cost of production. Investment or research credits, tax relief, fees or taxes imposed on manufacturers according to the amount and nature of the hazardous materials produced will reduce pollution. Such measures can help pay for treatment or disposal. They give companies an incentive to change their manufacturing processes so as to reduce hazardous waste production. Financial incentives for pollution make environmental cost internal, so that they can be taken into account when making production decisions.[38]

Although waste problems are global, the sources and sites of pollution are documented for US, Russia, Europe, China and each countries' cities. National emergency environmental clean up programs with costs and manpower requirements can be put into play. The economic effects will be to stimulate the economy, create jobs and produce boom times. Defense contractors have precisely the advanced technologies and the expertise required to solve the problems. Their entry will accelerate the restoration. The magnitude of the changes would vary considerably on an industry by industry basis.

Industrialized nations will have to make major and minor changes in their current practices. Developing nations will have to by pass older, less ecologically sound technologies and adopt new methods more compatible with their conditions. Projections indicate that to clean up smog, acid rain, nuclear radiation, toxic landfills and bring back the aquatic life to the waterways on our planet can take five years.

The US President and the Russian President can contact outstanding scientists and computer programmers and have them join in a special task force to find ways to decontaminate the thousands of deadly nuclear radiation waste sites. Universities, laboratories, think tanks and future institutes can be interconnected via two-way TV and find solutions to the Greenhouse Effect and the ozone emergency.

At the United Nations the Environment Committee can bring to the General Assembly a global fresh air and water plan which can be adopted. Standards would be established from ice cores taken from glaciers dated two thousand years ago, prior to the industrial revolution and the heavy burning of coal. 70,000 compounds would be quantified.[39]

Subsidies and loans can be made available to Third World countries to step up the renewal. Debt for nature swaps would add funds for conservation. The Montreal Protocol and other environmental treaties would impose a 5 year compliance. The 59 countries with Global Environment Monitoring stations[40] would expand to all and Antarctica. High tech instruments would be launched on new environment reconnaissance satellites.

The US President and the Russian President can lead delegations to Environmental Summits, as the historic UN Earth Summit in June 1992, in the Americas, Europe, Africa and Asia. Workable solutions and comprehensive recovery measures can be formulated and get underway. Russia can put part of the defense budget expenditures into national environmental clean up programs and target projects. In all cities millions of enthusiastic Russians can be actively involved in cleaning the rivers and lakes.

Factories which manufacture pollution technology will need to expand by 100 per cent in order to bring on line a sufficient number of new devices to meet the huge demands. The pollution control industry which employs 1.5 million people in Europe[41] would increase by 3 million jobs. The superpowers, multi-nationals and industrial giants can support industries in emission control by allowing various investment credits and write-offs.

AIR, LAND AND WATER - TODAY AND TOMORROW

The American President and his Environmental Secretary can attend the national Governors Conference, meet with the fifty state governors and coordinate comprehensive and sensible air, water and land policies. The elimination of air pollution in the US will save 40 billion dollars annually in health care and lost productivity.[42] Parliaments in South America and Africa can act on legislative bills to create billion dollar superfunds to eliminate the dangers. Mayors and city councils can adjust environmental laws to UN and World Health Organization standards. Within weeks nations can comply with comprehensive and stringent regulations to control the manufacture and release of toxic materials. India and China can launch massive clean up schemes for the waterways, canals and factories which should improve the health of billions of people.

Since time immemorial the falling rains and the changing seasons naturally cleansed the smoke and waste in the biosphere. But this is no longer true. Now in the global age, humans must manage the environment in ways which avoid the accumulation of materials contrary to health, either directly through toxic substances or indirectly through the damage to the farmland and oceans which support life.

Over the last fifty years of industrialization, especially in America and Europe, imprudent and short sighted policies, rather than malice, have produced a troublesome environmental legacy for everyone. Repeating the old mistakes certainly will not make matters better. Continuing the neglectful and reckless ways only pushes us closer to an ecological global collapse that nobody really wants. No one really knows, if once it starts, whether it can be turned around.

Steps can be taken to counteract rapid atmospheric change. A major decrease in the rate of fossil fuel combustion will slow the greenhouse warming, reduce smog, improve visibility and minimize acid deposition. Other steps can be targeted against particular gases, like methane whose emission can be reduced by instituting landfill operations that prevent its release.[43]

The environmental problems posed can be avoided by changes in disposal habits. Wastes from one industrial process will serve as the raw materials for another, thereby reducing the impact of industry on the environment. People sorting their trash to facilitate the recycling of paper, glass and plastics will simultaneously slow the filling of landfills and reduce the consumptions of scarce resources. The material used in beverage bottles is recycled in nine states that have mandatory deposit laws: California, Connecticut, Delaware, Maine, Massachusetts, Michigan, New York, Oregon and Vermont. Bottles collected in these states account for 150 million of the 750 million pounds of the material produced every year.[44] This can be expanded to all states.

In Russia, Japan and other countries special recycling industries in raw materials, scrap metals and reusable resources will need to expand. In Europe about 80 per cent of waste of all kinds can be put to use in one way or another.[45] Recycling of aluminium cans in the US could increase 20 times in ten years.[46]

Recent technological breakthroughs present considerable potential to reduce industry's global emission of pollutants. Japan, the US and Europe can expand the manufacturing and installation of monitoring sensors and micro electronics at sewage and treatment plants. Clean water and a stockpile of minerals will result. Stack gas cleanup and modern incineration in huge factory complexes in Chicago, Berlin, Osaka, and Bombay can effectively decompose or remove PCBs before they are released into the atmosphere. Trash combustion at landfills and home incinerators generates a variety of air pollutants which for the most part are controllable through a use of electro-static precipitators, fabric filters and lime scrubbers. Controlled sulfate emissions at utilities can produce sulfur as a by product larger than consumption levels.

The world's 400 million cars currently spew some 700 million tons of carbon into the atmosphere each year.[47] Automobile manufacturers, jet plane builders and train engineers can develop and produce renewable energy engines. Designers can rework existent motors. New nonpolluting fuels will be offered on the market. Space age engines will be invented. As a direct result, a corresponding cutback in smog, acid rain and air pollution will follow.

The long term solution will be to avoid the use of pesticides on insects and replace with genetic engineering, sterile techniques, biological control and resistance breeding. Subsidies in the developing countries on organic pesticides can range from 15 to 90 per cent.[48] By redirecting support to nonpesticide devices and techniques health hazards will diminish.

In Bulgaria the introduction of low and non-waste technologies would help reduce the discharge of industrial wastes by 5.5 million tons annually. In Hungary 6.5 million tons of industrial waste would be recycled.[49] To prevent further deterioration an array of successful national pilot programs, public and private, in the United States, Russia and worldwide will expand, train additional personnel and widen the conservation of the natural resources.

Recent medical breakthroughs in reproductive biology and genetics have already been adapted to save species. In an effort to increase the populations of some species reproductive biologists are implanting the embryos of zebras into horses and geneticists are breeding animals of the same species but from different zoos to produce offspring with more varied genetic makeups. The most endangered mammal in North America the black footed ferret was nearly lost. Science enabled the species to recover.[50]

Since trees are efficient absorbers of atmospheric carbon dioxide, enough could be planted by people to let nature do the work. About 720,000 square miles of new forest would remove one billion tons of carbon dioxide annually about a third of the problem. That's about 4.5 times the area of California. This could cool off the greenhouse effect.[51]

Due to lack of forest cover, massive flooding has occurred in India, prompting the Prime Minister to declare reforestation a priority in his current development agenda. With the assistance of the Agency for International Development 35 million trees were recently planted across the scorched and barren plains of Haiti.[52]

With new international support from policy makers and the general public the lives and health of billions can improve. Green brigades will be mobilized locally. The funding of Global Environmental Facility will be expanded. There will be every reason to have confidence in the future. The skies will be clear, the air smell fresh, and the water taste good in rivers around the planet. The rain forest will stabilize. Commercial fish catches in the oceans can once again increase. Animal and plant species will be staging recoveries, the blue whales in the Pacific, rhinoceros in India and mountain gorillas in tropical Africa. The Global Renaissance will be underway.

Almost five decades of worsening problems have made it clear that half measures offer unrealistic hope. Short term actions, even if well intentioned, will not be adequate to end the deadly pollution crisis. If the acid rain, smog alerts, chemical explosions, oil spills, sewage releases and nuclear accidents continue then the next ten or twenty years will witness an irreversible environmental collapse.

The superpowers are the world's foremost producers of oil, chemicals, iron, steel and heavy machinery, and consequently the largest

AIR, LAND AND WATER - TODAY AND TOMORROW

polluters of industrial waste. To continue the old course would be dangerous and unwise. People in the US, Russia, Democratic, Socialist and Communist nations by not polluting, recycling and voting will terminate the air, water and land disaster, and restore our Earthly paradise.

CHAPTER 3

POPULATION - PROMISE
OR PERIL

10,000 years ago people gathered into small Neolithic settlements. There were from five to 10 million human beings then, not enough to exercise much influence on the ecosystem within which they lived as hunters and farmers. That situation prevailed for most of the next 100 centuries. Only in the past few decades have humans brought about changes comparable in magnitude to those wrought by nature during long epochs of geological time.[1]

The same wellsprings of human inventiveness that is so transforming the Earth has also given us the unprecedented understanding of how the planet works, how our present activities threaten its workings and how we can intervene to improve the prospects for its sustainable development.

The modern world is a paradox. Human civilization in many regards has advanced to a high state. Nations provide a standard of living, great capacity to take care of their people, broad possibilities for education and an enlightened morality. However, we haven't yet controlled global population which effects development, the fragile environment, finite resources and the future.

Humans are increasing by more than 10,000 an hour, 250,000 daily and nearly 90 million this coming year.[2] On our small planet, which is 70 per cent ocean and 30 per cent land, the population is exploding. Each new person born puts additional pressure on the food supply, available land, housing, energy and waste.

Global population is outgrowing the biological systems and outstripping croplands, fisheries, forests and grassland which we depend upon for survival. It is outpacing the capacity of a number of developing countries to provide for their economic and social well being. Natural resources are depleting faster than they can be regenerated. Productivity is reduced and development undermined.[3]

Consequently, today 40,000 children under five will unnecessarily die due to starvation, malnutrition and disease.[4] In the next 12 months 340 to 730 million people, particularly in Asia and Africa, will suffer from hunger and chronic malnutrition.[5] In a decade world population will require a level of agricultural output some 50 to 60 per cent higher than now. Demand for food in developing countries will double.[6]

Meanwhile, more and more people are moving to cities, causing extraordinary urban concentration around the world. Before the advent of modern transport and the international grain trade, the size of a city was determined by its ability to command the agricultural surplus of farmland, usually in neighboring areas. All that has changed now. Mexico City and Caracas have grown by exchanging oil for food. New Delhi has expanded by virtue of its rail network, and Calcutta has grown due to water transport. In cities that have nothing to exchange foreign aid has intervened to mitigate hunger and in so doing increased population further. No longer dependent on local products to trade for food and other necessities, cities around the world are expanding rapidly.[7]

Unless population growth levels off by the 21st century or before eleven countries will exceed fifty million. Nine nations, including Pakistan and Mexico, will have more than one hundred million. India will be well over one billion people.[8] Cities and villages will continue to expand and conditions deteriorate. Projections indicate more than 6 billion humans will inhabit our small crowded planet, nearly a billion more than today (Chart 9).

However, one billion more people can virtually eat all the known

GLOBAL RENAISSANCE

CHART 9

**GROWTH OF
WORLD POPULATION**

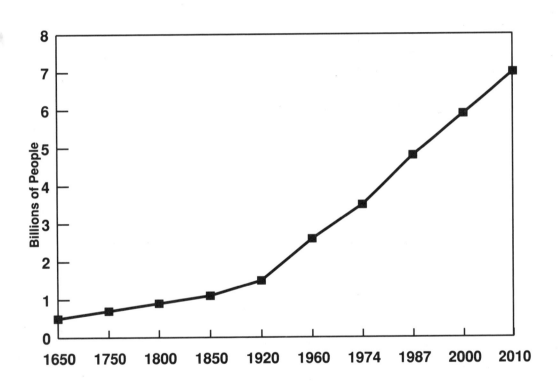

Source: UNFPA

food supplies, producing an irreversible cycle of famine, starvation and death. If this happens America, Europe and Russia will be struggling for survival. This will continue until a common global policy aimed at a sustained population is implemented. For thousands of years humans grew gradually at a steady pace, as language, society and civilization simultaneously developed. In 1650 world population numbered about 500 million. From a total of about one billion in 1830, it increased five times in less than 160 years. It took nearly a century for humankind to grow to the second billion, but only some 35 years (1964) for the third to swell our numbers, 10 years (1974) for the fourth billion, 13 years (1987) for the fifth, and the sixth billion mark is expected to be reached around the turn of the century. This rapid growth presents a great challenge, but also constitutes great risks to humankind. The demands being made on our finite natural resources are greater than ever before.[9]

However, in the last two centuries each important upsurge in the number of people followed a major invention or change that made more food available. Among the great achievements were advances in farming, construction of irrigation canals and the invention of machines to do the field work of humans. Families grew until they absorbed the new supply of food, energy and resources. The process continued until there wasn't enough land. Then as a result there was less to go around in the community, the quality of life deteriorated and famines became widespread.

In the 1980s pressures were beginning to build and strains on various systems starting to show up. When population reached 5 billion the per capita production of mutton and forest products peaked. As the population explosion continued human needs began to surpass the productive capacity of many local ecological systems, farmlands, pastures and the waterways.

GLOBAL RENAISSANCE

Presently, overgrazing is common place in Africa and Asia. Forests are shrinking in many countries. Over logging is directly related to the demand from ever expanding populations for building material, firewood, additional land and foreign capital. Heavy floods caused by deforestation have recently led Thailand to ban all logging.[10]

Throughout most of human existence there were more fish in the rivers, lakes and oceans than could ever hope to be consumed. But by the late 1980s this changed when the per capita catch decreased.[11] Pressure on stocks in certain areas amounted to overfishing. In regions close to the industrial areas of the northern hemisphere resulted in a decline in the size and quality of some species of fish and the increasing scarcity of others. Overfishing has led to a sharp drop in catches of cod and herring in particular in the northeast Atlantic.[12] Sub-Saharan Africa's cereal import needs are estimated to exceed last year's by some 25 per cent with food-aid requirements rising by an estimated 43 per cent.[13]

The global problems that arose this century as world population began to explode may seem insignificant compared with those in store if human numbers go from 6 to 7 billion and beyond. Unless birth control changes are accelerated, Egypt will have to squeeze an additional 12 million people into the crowded and over farmed Nile Valley in the next decade. The United States will need food and resources for an added 14 million and Russia 12 million critically changing exports and surplus. Indonesia is expected to have 29 million more to sustain. Bangladesh badly overcrowded and existing on a threadbare margin of survival, would have to find the means of supporting another 31 million. Nigeria struggling to feed and maintain political and economic order would have to cope with 46 million more. China will have another 162 million.[14]

If national family planning programs based on the United Nations population policy of replacement (one child per person) aren't put in place immediately then millions of people born in the years ahead will needlessly starve to death. Food reserves will be drawn down to dangerous levels. In the US, Russia, Europe and Japan rationing will go into effect. The calorie intake will drastically be cut back for children and the elderly. Billions of people will suffer from malnutrition. As armies battle for food, wars will most likely break out on all the continents.

Throughout history villages and cities that were overpopulated eventually perished. Now we live in an age when a population explosion threatens the entire planet. The US President and the Russian President have to face up to our common reality and provide the needed statesmanship so crucial for these dangerous times. Clearly, additional innovative birth control measures, including those of an exceptional nature, are urgently called for.

In a matter of days the two presidents can be seen on TV landing in jetcopters at health clinics in the capitol cities of India and China. With prime ministers they can inaugurate family planning programs. The arms shipments by the superpowers that had been scheduled to allies can be suspended and a portion of the trillion dollars appropriated for health clinics, medical technicians and birth control devices.

There is a striking unmet need for family planning programs in developing countries (Chart 10). In Africa only 17 per cent of the women are practising contraception, in South Asia 40 per cent and in Latin America 60 per cent. If women who wanted no more children were able to stop the number of births would be reduced today by 22 per cent. Without family planning the 1990 population of India, China and developing countries would have been 700 million more people. India alone saved 742 billion dollars on health care costs and education by averting births.[15]

GLOBAL RENAISSANCE

CHART 10

CONTRACEPTION/INFANT
MORTALITY

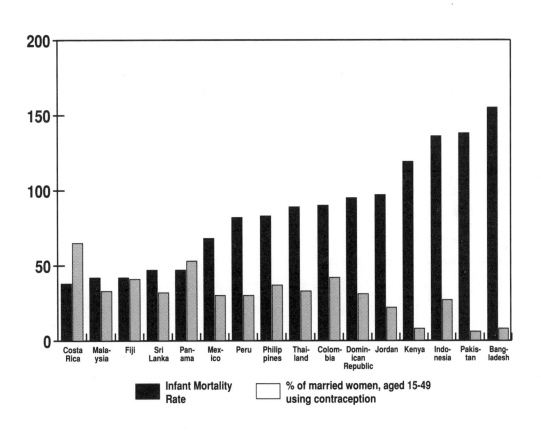

Source: UNFPA Annual Report

POPULATION - PROMISE OR PERIL

Population stability, low fertility and a contraceptive prevalence rate are attainable in Africa, Asia and worldwide. The cost will be about 9 billion dollars a year by the end of the century to governments, contraceptive users and the international community.[16] If greater financial and technical assistance are allocated then the population will level off at 6 billion.

In less than a month Nigeria, Ethiopia and other African governments, where the birth rate is the most serious, can direct 10-20 per cent of the old armaments budgets, billions of dollars, into fertility control measures. At the UN Headquarters in New York international family planning services can be coordinated via telecommunication and computers. The 2,849 projects would be increased significantly.[17]

In South America a Population Conferences can be held with thousands of doctors, nurses, midwifes, experts and officials attending. The meetings can be broadcast via satellite to all countries. Decisions of the next five years can substantially affect turning the crisis around. If so in cities and villages on all the continents, the economic and social results will be immense. As the number of people stabilize men, women and children will no longer suffer starvation, hunger and malnutrition. There will be enough food to go around. Yearly the standard of living will rise. A Renaissance life will come about.

In North America and Europe nations can emphasize those family planning customs most appropriate to their own unique cultures. Radio, television and newspapers will inform a large rural population and billions of residents in cities to an array of practices. The US and Russia can provide teachers, technical aid, birth control supples and jet transports to Third World countries. In the coming year conditions can change more quickly and favorably than most people might first expect. In the next thirty days congresses can transfer the doctors, nurses, medical personnel, vehicles and hospitals out of the military and into an expanded national health care service. Buildings at former army, air force and navy bases in all countries can be turned into family planning centers.

The birth control programs established in Asian nations the past two decades can serve as models for other countries. Information and access to contraceptives have been major causes of declining fertility. In China, Indonesia, Thailand and South Korea crude birth rates declined from 25 to 60 per cent. In Tunisia the rates dropped about twice as fast in the decade after the program began. The birth rate in Mauritania was nearly 40 per 1,000 when a program was initiated and dropped to below 25 per 1,000 during the first eight years. Family planning programs account for from 10 to 40 per cent of declines in birth rates.[18]

Indonesia's National Family Planning Coordinating Board has established more than 40,000 village distribution centers for contraceptive devices and information, mostly in Java and Bali. They provide social centers where people receive free contraceptives. Educational programs promote the notion that a family should be small, happy and prosperous. The national family planning jingle plays when a train passes a railway crossing. Religious leaders give lectures on contraception at the local mosques. Islam accepts birth control and at five o'clock every afternoon sirens wail to remind women to take their pill. Couples that practice birth control have increased nearly fifty fold.[19]

The lowering of the birth rate can be brought about by strong government and community support, education and the dissemination of contraceptives. For some of the countries in Asia, South America and especially Africa in which family planning has not been successful, new administrations can focus more time and resources to solving the impending problem. Most of the less developed nations are now at the point where sizable portions of their populations want smaller families than has traditionally been the norm. Couples need to be provided with the widest possible choices of methods.

Throughout farming villages and cities in Pakistan, Paraguay and Tanzania thousands of new mobile health vans from the military can provide birth control services, medical check-ups for expecting mothers and pre-natal care. In Kenya men and women of child bearing age could have one or two children, rather than four or five, and consequently a more prosperous life.

Burma and Chad by implementing a full scale family program assure that overpopulation is never reached. In so doing, the standard of living will be raised, housing and health care increased and the material world of television and cars made more available in the future. A dramatic drop in the Bangladesh birth rate due to a marked decline in fertility can result from making a variety of simple and low cost contraceptives available to everyone.

Parents who have more than two children will be taxed for the additional expense to the nation. As a result the population will stabilize. The additional food can be used to bolster diets.

Half the 500,000 maternal deaths which occur each year in pregnancy and child bearing could be prevented with changes in timing, spacing and numbers of pregnancies which in turn can be affected by family planning services. 25 per cent of under five mortality could be eliminated if mothers waited until eighteen years to have the first child, spaced births at least twenty four months apart and avoided pregnancy after having four children or after the age of thirty five. This leads to lower numbers of children.[20]

A widespread program of legal abortions across Russia and Japan can commonly be performed and decrease unwanted pregnancies. The share of the world population living in societies where safe abortion is readily available can increase.

In Egypt vasectomy operations in clinics and out patient hospitals, taking a few minutes, for the educated and peasants alike, can become widely used and have a considerable effect in halting unwanted children. Energetic national campaigns with public service announcements and billboards around Brazil will result in millions of couples registering their interest in family planning and getting involved with birth control methods. In Bolivia the installation of condom machines in village general stores and apothecaries will facilitate ready access to contraceptives and result in a decline in the population growth.

The poorest countries on the globe with the highest birth rates can be provided with contraceptives rather than weapons from the superpowers, Europe and other nations. This will in turn limit the number of children born and allow a new way of life to blossom.

Among the most recent and promising contraceptive developments is Norplant which can be implanted under the skin and is effective for up to five years. Intrauterine devices and injections of Depo-Provera, a synthetic hormone are more convenient in that they only require occasional visits to health clinics.[21]

In neighborhood storefronts in Moscow, Madrid, London and hundreds of other cities in Europe, Planned Parenthood organizations can expand and provide men and women with birth control literature, counseling and devices like diaphragms and cervical caps. In all communities Universities, colleges and high schools will need to teach sex education. People will have to practise safe sex.

In the United States scientists might invent new forms of condoms, intercervical devices, foams, low dose orals, vaccines, advanced IUD's, post-coital tablets and utilize genetic engineering. In a few years contraceptive manufacturing output can double with massive shipments to developing countries.

Throughout history families and societies have made use of contraceptives. Some methods developed in earlier times are still widely used. In Egyptian writings dating back nearly 4,000 years primitive diaphragms appear. Later discs of oiled silk paper were introduced in China and Japan, while Europeans employed linen clothes, wafers of molded wax, and sea sponges. The Bible mentions an ancient technique Coitus Interruptus.[22]

The use of mechanical contraceptives on any relevant scale began with the discovery of vulcanizing rubber in 1843. This allowed the mass manufacturing of prophylactics. The first IUD's made of silkworm gut in the shape of a ring were introduced in Germany in 1909. The first vasectomy was performed more than 300 years ago, but began to be used routinely in 1925.[23] Rapid advances of knowledge in reproductive physiology during the last 30 years, have led to new methods of controlling human fertility, particularly the pill for women and men. Around our globe appropriate long term solutions to the population crisis are readily available.

People ultimately will become aware of how their own childbearing effects the future ecological stability of their country and of the planet. If the economy is undermined by overpopulation, this cannot but depress economic growth. People will come to understand that it is preferable to have a few children of high quality rather than to have many children who will be uneducated and unemployed.[24]

Today, with modern birth control techniques, the UN Population Program and the support of the superpowers there can be an end to the population explosion. However, if population policies continue at the status quo, this will perpetuate an inherent crisis. Politicians and officials can't continue to pay lip service to change, while the reality of the problem worsens. The delays and insufficient actions by governments will continue to be found at the gravesites of millions of innocent people who die from starvation and malnutrition. Overpopulation is the result of incomplete policies which can be corrected.

The difficulties in bringing population growth to a halt quickly must be weighed against the cost of failing to do so in time to avoid a collapse of the planet's major biological systems. Pressure on resources from the explosion in the numbers of people has reached a point where national efforts to cope with the on going catastrophe will not succeed without a concerted global effort to slam on the demographic brakes.

To a considerable measure how the challenge of population is resolved determines how economic development turns out. Looking one or five or even fifty years ahead, rather than month to month, as has been customary in the past, we can see that a prerequisite for a prosperous future and a lasting peace are a stable global populace. The US President, the Russian President and other leaders are at a crossroads and have to make the proper choices immediately.

Population and health are interlinked. Globally too many people have put a serious strain on the limited health care in nations. In some regions families have never seen a doctor. In Africa 40 per cent of all mothers give birth unattended by trained personnel. In South America 50 per cent of pregnant women are unable to get tetanus immunization. In South East Asia local health care is not within one hour's walk or travel for 40 per cent of the population.[25]

In countries faced with increasing industrial pollution, the United States, Russia, Europe and Japan, environmental illnesses, cancer, heart disease and tuberculosis have caused a crisis in some medical systems. For the vast majority of the urban poor access to basic health care is difficult.

The economic development of a country is clearly limited when one out of five children dies before completing one year of life, when a high proportion of children suffer from stunted growth due to malnutrition, when a lifetime can be shortened by disease, or when a person is beset by disability and illness at what is the most productive age.[26]

In the capitals of many developing countries ultra-modern hospitals have facilities for open heart surgery and organ transplants, while outside the city limits children still die of tetanus or diarrhea because basic services and supplies are lacking. Overcrowding and the deterioration of urban health facilities are evident. Even in the developed countries decaying inner city areas are growing, and the health and social needs of the urban poor are becoming a serious challenge.[27]

Dramatic differences in life expectancy exist with 78 years in Sweden and 42 years in Afghanistan.[28] In Africa life expectancy at birth is still below 50 years in a majority of countries. In Latin America and the Caribbean only 10% of the population have a life expectancy at birth of 60 years or older.[29] The United States is 72 for men and 79 for women.[30] In developing countries infant mortality rates are about eight times higher and female life expectancy about a third shorter, than in industrial countries.[31]

Malaria remains a major public health problem in many countries. Malaria is an important cause of child mortality, especially in tropical Africa. The increasing efforts to control the disease have been hampered by the emergence of mosquitoes resistant to the more readily available insecticides. 56 per cent of the world population lives in countries or areas where malaria continues to be a public health problem.

The population at risk from Malaria is over 2 billion. Annually there are 227 million malaria parasitic infections. 2.6 million malaria cases are reported. Southeast Asia accounts for about half of the world total.[32]

200 million people are infected with schistosomiasis, and 500 to 600 million are exposed to the threat of infection. This disease is the result of heavy parasite loads in children. The chronic, debilitating illness seen in adults is the outcome of heavy childhood infestation. The geographical range is from China, the Philippines and Indonesia through the Arabian Peninsula, North Africa to South America and certain Caribbean islands.[33]

In the very small countries of Bhutan, Maldives and Seychelles, a real shortage of professional manpower persists since candidates for training and even the training facilities themselves are lacking.[34]

Globally there is a serious shortage of doctors, dentists, pharmacists, nurses, midwifes, medics, lab technicians, sanitation personnel and community health workers. The private and public training institutions and medical colleges vary greatly from country to country, but for the most part are inadequate for the critical needs.

Government budgets in the 1970s, 80s and 90s in all developing countries dropped for health care. In sub-Saharan Africa real expenditure decreased which meant that the enormous gap in per capita spending on human resources between industrial and developing countries has been widening rather than closing.[35]

Drug shortages are common in public clinics. Zambia's free government health services ceased for lack of basic supplies. There are long waiting times in government facilities up to five hours in Uganda and eight hours in Nigeria.[36]

Most current public health spending goes to nonessential drugs and expensive services provided largely by hospitals. Inexpensive health measures in terms of the cost of each death averted such as immunization and prenatal care are not as well financed[37] (Chart 11).

Without affordable access to basic health care the middle class worldwide has great difficulties and the poor in developing countries have little chance of improving their prospects. Currently the health of billions of people in the world is unacceptable and will worsen year by year. Until the US President, the Russian President, the Secretary-General and national leaders provide leadership so that the United Nations goal of health for all by the year 2000 will be achieved.

This will accelerate immunization against diphtheria, tetanus, whooping-cough, measles, polio, and tuberculosis. Local health care facilities will be built within one hour's walk or travel with at least 20 essential drugs. Personnel will be trained for attending pregnancy and childbirth, and caring for children up to 1 year.

The superpowers and other countries can allocate a portion of the 1 trillion dollars diverted from the military and boost national health care services. Investment in human resources is critical for the alleviation of needless suffering and early death. Currently about 5 per cent of GNP is spent on health.[38] When 50 per cent is added to the public health budgets the sick can get better, those near death can live and children will have full lives. Inexpensive measures of immunization, oral rehydration, breast feeding, birth spacing and the introduction of hygiene could do much.[39] By investing an additional 100 billion dollars annually our human family will be brought back from near death to good health and long life.

For a brief moment during civil conflict in one country a cease-fire was declared to permit a nationwide immunization campaign for 300,000 children. Central American countries, in spite of their political and ideological differences were able to come together to elaborate a Central American health plan using health as a bridge for peace.[40]

countries, industrial and developing. The malaise is worldwide. The fault lies in that we are living in a global age, but attempting to solve problems nationally. The US President and the Russian President wield extraordinary power over nations, people and major political systems. The superpowers and their allies account for 68 per cent of the world GNP.[56] Enlightened political commitment by these two leaders and others, along with vigorous coordination, the boosting of staffs and global computer monitoring will be keys to achieving health for all by the year 2000. The future of health care will largely depend on the extent to which people and governments in Washington, Moscow, Europe, Japan, China, India and elsewhere address the health policy issues.

CHAPTER 4

FOOD - FEAST OR FAMINE

To feed adequately both the present population and 1 billion additional people by the beginning of the next century, it will be necessary to increase food production by 3 to 4 per cent annually. However, increasing food production by unsustainable and unsafe means will bring worse problems. Sustainable agricultural growth demands concerted action by governments, international agencies, communities and individuals with investment in agricultural machinery, use of environmentally safe fertilizers, pesticides and alternative fuels.[1]

Currently, millions of people are dying of hunger and starvation and hundreds of millions are trapped in a cycle of malnutrition and inadequate diets. When global population is stabilized vis-a-vis birth control the level of food security needs to be high enough to sustain people during local or global disasters due to weather, locust infestation or crop plagues.

Today in groceries and butcher shops in Russia, the commonwealth and Eastern Europe with a population of over 400 million[2] the food, can goods and fruits on shelves or in transit amount to approximately a 3 to 7 day supply. Meat is scarce.

In developing countries famine is affecting some 45 million

people. 1 billion men, women and children are suffering from some form of malnutrition and food insecurity.[3] Last years yields fell in Western and Eastern Europe. A significant decline in wheat, rice and coarse grains in Brazil is responsible for the overall fall in output levels in South America for the second consecutive year.[4]

Twenty years ago most of Africa was self-sufficient in food. In the 1980s about 140 million Africans were dependent on imported grain.[5] Today this continent's food supply situation remains the most precarious. Ethiopia, Mozambique, Sudan and 14 other African countries are currently experiencing severe food shortages. Over 4 million tons of emergency food assistance is required, more than that for the last two years combined.[6] The human food condition particularly in developing countries continues to worsen. One out of three children under the age of five are malnourished.[7]

World cereal stocks, working and emergency, are at 17 to 18 per cent of consumption. However, nearly all of the increase in global carry over stocks is expected to occur in the developed countries, particularly the United States and Canada which are the breadbaskets of the planet. As stocks are only minimally above safe levels, the outcome of this year's harvests will again be critical.[8]

The growing hunger of this decade is not only causing great human suffering and waste of human and economic resources now. But it also jeopardizes the opportunities of future generations by impairing the physical and mental development of today's children.

In the US, Russia, Europe, Japan and industrialized farming systems petro-fertilizers and pesticides play an important part. However, these chemicals are found in groundwater and may cause ailments including cancer.[9] 60 to 90 per cent of the chemicals sprayed on crops are used to beautify produce, not to improve its quality. Only 10 per cent of the 35,000 pesticides have been tested for potential health effects.[10]

In many regards, even those who live in affluent societies, if there were extended catastrophes, the limited stored food supply would not last long. Around our global village the low stocks of grains in silos, warehouses and elevators indicates that humankind's survival is precarious.

In order to boost global food security particularly in these troubled times tractors, seed reserves, processing plants, infrastructures and most importantly storage facilities worldwide need to be expanded substantially. The US and Russia, rather than spending millions a minute on weapons and buying insecurity, economic and social ruin, should allocate billions for needed farm equipment, irrigation dams and agrarian reforms. Undoubtedly, these changes will help in solving the global food crisis, as well as lower the cost at supermarkets and build up national grain reserves. New policies will enhance the long-term development of South American, Eastern European and Asian nations in becoming self sufficient in agricultural production.

The transition to a modern farming world might be difficult. However, it can be expedited by the US President, Russian President and all other leaders. If the global agenda of the superpowers and other nations included stockpiling grain instead of weapons then in a few years our world community would find itself with a new globo-agrarian storage system and plenty of food. This in turn will make living in the Global Renaissance healthy and special.

However, due to the Ozone holes, the Greenhouse Effect and mans' uncontrollable plundering of the planet, this winter may very well see record cold temperatures, forcing an unusually short spring. Of the wheat and grain planted only a small percentage would actually be harvested. This would force the world food production to plummet with the poorest performance in a century. The Far East and Africa will most likely suffer the worst setback owing to the weakest monsoons in years with per capita food production falling 50 per cent.

Europeans might very well find themselves living with food shortages worse than World War II. Russia might try to make massive grain purchases from stocks in the US and Canada. But these strategic reserves would already be drawn down. For Americans and Russians, like most others, food will be scarce and rationed. Villages throughout China and India will experience the worst starvation in thousands of years with hundreds of millions of people dying.

The troubles would be scarcely over when early snowstorms and unusually cold temperatures destroy much of the remaining fields on all the continents. As a consequence almost overnight global hunger will be the worst in history. Massive marches and food riots would follow in the streets. Military ships most likely will escort fishing vessels in the open seas to protect the small catches. Due to the scarce world food reserves Sweden, Britain, the US and Russia will probably go to war. The results would be millions killed in combat and billions of people starve to death.

The superpower presidents and government leaders in most nations conduct business, as if nothing has happened in the last year to five years to change course immediately. The current uncoordinated short term food approaches will not solve the hunger and lack of stored grain supplies. Every day the answers are delayed the problems not only grow, but compound and become more deadly.

Without a revival of the world economy, there is little prospect for a reduction of malnutrition and poverty, let alone their elimination. Agricultural recovery depends on future policy actions. Today the US and Russian Presidents can go on national television and outline the new initiatives and specific programs to alleviate the world food crisis. In private conversations they can assist and leverage allies and trading partners to move as quickly as possible. Available grain from the United States, Australia, and Argentina can be airlifted via US and Russian jumbo jets to starving people.

In a few days nations can begin to launch practical projects covering land reform, crop storage, pesticides, fertilizers, topsoil, new foods, high-tech farming, aquaculture and clean water. Many new and old agricultural methods will find their way into widespread use. Free market policies and institutions will induce farmers to adopt new technologies and management practices. To offset increasing scarcities of land, water and environmental resources, a steady supply of farming improvements will be needed in the future.

Achieving sustainable global agriculture will clearly require the long-term support of our commons, the land, water and genetic diversity of species. Not only must the food supply expand, it must expand in a way that does not destroy the natural environment. For that to happen a steady stream of new technologies that minimize erosion, desertification, salinization of the soil and other damage must be introduced.[11]

The Third World can redirect their national investments to target agriculture as a top priority. The foreign aid of the United States, Russia, Europe and Japan can increase the available funds. In five years this will enable developing countries to substantially increase their rural production and achieve food security.

In a month the United Nations Food Conference can be meeting with delegates in Singapore in workshops pointing out ways for combating hunger in Asia. Non-governmental organizations, major banking institutions and multinational agribusiness could coordinate a wide range of programs producing a boom period for trade and commerce.

National agriculture research establishments and the 13 institutes in the Consultative Group on International Agricultural Research can expand. Scientists will breed and genetically engineer new species of plants increasing nutrition and crop production.

Empty factories, particularly in America, Europe and Russia, can be turned into assembly lines manufacturing high tech agricultural equipment for domestic and export use. Dockworkers will load ships with mini tractors instead of tanks bound for Third World countries. Employment in industrial cities will increase to fill the needed jobs. The gross national product in every nation will go up. Optimism among people will be widespread.

As soon as a country met the UN population standards, then low interest long term loans for food projects will be arranged and brought on line. In Central America and Southeast Asia plows, pumps and planters can be unloaded from former navy vessels. Local training schools for men and women can be set up. In China wilderness territory along rivers can be deeded to people to farm and homestead in an historic agrarian reform program.

To its ecological advantage, multiple cropping can sharply increase yields. In the American Midwest farmers are growing corn with sugar beets. The yield of sugar increased by 11 per cent. The greater sunlight penetration and more rapid replenishment of carbon dioxide to the corn's leaves increased the yield of corn by 150 per cent. Where there is multiple cropping pests, weeds, insects and pathogens cannot as easily adapt themselves to a single set of conditions and therefore do not increase as quickly.[12]

In Europe, North Africa, Russia, the Great Plains regions of Canada and the US trees are used in a multiple cropping system. Windbreaks made up of trees protect growing crops from the drying effect of wind and mechanical damage. Multiple cropping employed in Central

America calls for growing maize, beans and squash together which enriches the soil and increases the harvests.[13]

The spread of irrigation contributed between 50 to 60 percent of the massive increase in agricultural output of the developing countries in recent decades.[14] Massive projects on major rivers on all the continents could expand irrigation globally. But irrigation water can contain as much as 3.5 tons of salt per 1,000 cubic meters or about 13 tons per acre. The plants take up very little. Most of it is left behind in the soil as the water evaporates. Technical means for dealing with salinization are known. The salt must be flushed out of the root zone by applying excess water.[15] Along the ocean desalinization plants in Israel and the United States take the salt out of the water. These stations can be commercially expanded in years to come and provide an endless supply of fresh water for irrigation and drinking.

In the many parts of the world where the land is threatened by erosion measures to remedy the problem will be undertaken. In the Middle East the land is shaped to permit rain to run off large upland areas into collection devices. Gravity-flow irrigation systems, the most widely used type, can be improved by laser leveling, maximizing flooding and minimizing water usage.[16]

Restoring one of the Earth's life-supporting systems, its soil, will require heavy capital investments and strong commitments by political leaders. American farmers are loosing 3 billion tons of topsoil annually from water and wind, some 2 billion tons in excess of tolerable levels. Converting 40 million acres of highly erodible cropland to grassland or woodland will cost the US Treasury 2 billion dollars per year once the full area is retired. The erosion will decline from 29 tons per acre to two tons. Excessive erosion would be reduced by over 1 billion tons. Annual expenditures of roughly 3 billion dollars would be required for the

GLOBAL RENAISSANCE

United States to stabilize the soils on its cropland.[17]

Global expenditures to protect the cropland base would total some 24 billion dollars per year. Although this is obviously a large sum, as an investment in future food supplies for a world expecting billions of more people, it is one that humanity can ill afford not to make.[18]

Across America and Russia old missile silos, weapons arsenals, and underground civil defense shelters can be turned into grain storage sites, and linked with computers to national and international food reserve centers. The North Pole and the South Pole, our planet's natural refrigeration system, can see massive storage pits excavated and filled with surplus corn, rice and barley unloaded from jet transports and giant ice breakers. Projections indicate in the global food storage network thousands of new local grain elevators and storage warehouses need to be constructed.

Five thousand years ago it seemed as though humans would never run out of land. Then the world numbered in the hundreds of millions, and was thought to be flat and endless. The early farming clans, as well as the Chinese, Indian, Egyptian, Hebrew, Greek and Roman civilizations, from which succeeding ones developed, remedied food shortages by bringing additional land into cultivation. When food production, as in the Nile river valley, successfully outdistanced population then there was a flowering of the arts. The last thousand years has seen a gradual replacement of people working in fields with horses and oxen.

At the turn of this century the planet was on the threshold of an agricultural revolution the likes of which were almost beyond imagination. The use of oil and the invention of the gasoline engine, coupled with the factory assembly line produced new automated vehicles, tractors, harvesters and trucks, which began to replace animals. The land was planted with new scientifically developed high yield grains. The crops were sprayed with pesticides from airplanes for insects. The water was fortified with high dosages of chemical fertilizers. The farming work force dropped dramatically (Chart 12). Currently in the US, Australia, Canada and a few advanced nations 2 to 3 per cent of the population are required for food production.

In the 1950s through the 80s the Green Revolution spread to Mexico, Pakistan, the Philippines and Indonesia. The stocks of grains rose. However, population not only kept pace but exploded. Television screens filled with the sights of starving children. Today, there is no reason for people to starve to death or go hungry. Nearly all countries have the potential to expand cultivated areas (Chart 13).

The caloric needs of over 8 billion people is equal to the quantity of food the world's cattle consume. To supply one person with a meat habit food for a year requires three and a quarter acres. To supply a vegetarian requires only one sixth of an acre. A given acreage can feed twenty times as many people as it could with the standard American diet. One acre of land can grow 20,000 pounds of potatoes or if used to grow cattle, can produce less than 165 pounds of beef. If Americans were to reduce their meat consumption by only ten percent, it would free over 12 million tons of grain annually for human consumption. That, by itself, would be enough to adequately feed 60 million human beings who will starve to death on the planet.[19]

However, in Latin America there are millions of acres of fertile lands which might be brought into ranching. The production of prime beef can increase making the continent a leading exporter of this source of protein. In Texas, Wyoming and Arizona two thousand pound beefalos, a cross between cattle and buffalo can be bred utilizing artificial insemination and cloning. The herds might be built up and shipped to other countries.

GLOBAL RENAISSANCE

CHART 12

WORK FORCE

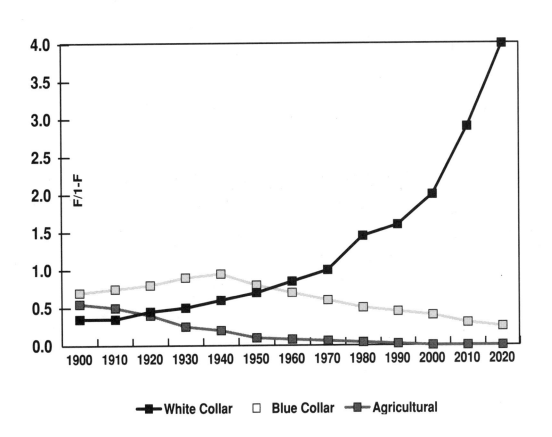

Source: "Recollecting the Future," 1988; Hugh B. Stewart

FOOD—FEAST OR FAMINE

CHART 13

**LAND USE AND
RESERVES**

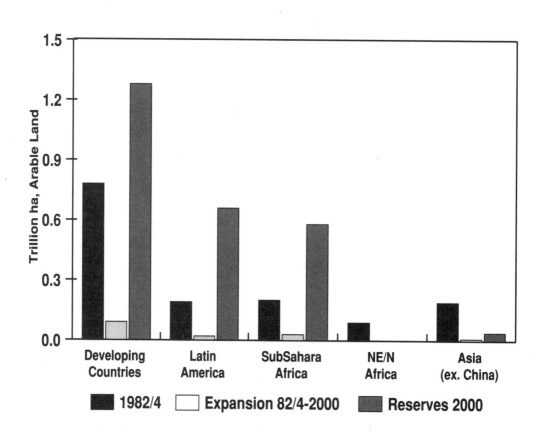

Source: "World Agriculture Toward 2000," FAO

GLOBAL RENAISSANCE

The intensive growing of giant grasshoppers, beetles and other insects in technically monitored pollution free ranches in Florida, Puerto Rico and Indonesia offers a high protein source of nutrition and annual yields two to three times more than other types of food.

On rivers in Asia new irrigation dams and aqueducts can be constructed, extending the arable acreage, increasing the grain harvest and bolstering diets. In deserts airplanes can seed clouds bringing undreamed of rainfall. In tropical Africa water pumps, steel plows, hand tools and solar tractors will accelerate the building of new farms.

Data processing centers in government capitols with high speed computers will record and project food production, storage capacity, and consumption trends. They will be connected to UN Headquarters in New York. Orbiting satellites will telephoto and inventory the exact condition of the world's crops daily and weekly. Simultaneously, livestock in fields and schools of fish will be surveyed. The weather satellite network will monitor and act as an early warning system for droughts and Arctic freezes.

Americans, Russians and billions of others in cities can plant new mini-gardens on roofs and in backyards. Skyscraper greenhouses can grow vegetables in abundance. Corporations, private firms, churches and universities can make available land for commons and mini-farms. From Boston to Los Angeles, tens of thousands of unused lots will be turned into cultivated plots yielding fruits, crops and flowers.

Pyramid hot houses can be in widespread commercial use in metropolitan centers. These provide a new fully controlled farming environment. High yields will occur because crops are scientifically grown and pushed from two to four harvests a year. Only minimum amounts of water and nutrients are required, and it's free of pests. The annual harvest per quarter acre for some food plants would increase thirty per cent. However, this approach results in relatively high production costs, making it feasible for only a few countries.

Trickle or drip irrigation gained wide acceptance in Israel, the US and other countries in the 1970s and is now being introduced around the world. Trickle systems deliver water directly to a small area next to an individual plant. The water is carried by tubing, either buried or on the surface, usually a nozzle emitter releases the small amount of water. The waste water is recycled back into the farm's irrigation system and strategically reapplied to the fields at times and in ways that minimize the effects of the salts carried in it.[20]

Composting has been practiced since the beginning of history. Humus, a kind of soil conditioner, is produced from the decomposition of organic materials.[21] Manure, mulches, leaves, wood chips, natural fertilizers and fecal matter are used in farming around the Earth and can be expanded substantially.

Plants can be biologically engineered to produce nitrogen in the soil. A prime candidate for such a transformation is corn. Biotechnology makes it possible to manipulate the genetic material of this organism directly. Laboratories will eventually make the breakthroughs. The demand for petrol-fertilizers would be greatly reduced.[22]

In New England at the Woodshole Oceanographic Institute processed sewage can be used to grow marine algae which in turn is fed to clams, oysters and lobsters. All over the world sewage might be treated and then used in large scale aquaculture projects. In the US, China and Holland tens of thousands of fish farms on small canals and huge computer monitored ponds can be expanded. Catfish, carp and trout will be hatched and raised feeding millions.

The lives of small farmers near Manila in the Philippines have recently taken a dramatic turn for the better. The farmers are practicing organic farming ensuring healthier and more sustainable harvests. With the old methods every six sacks of petro fertilizer produced 50 to 75 sacks of rice. Now with new techniques chemicals are eliminated and rice is grown naturally. The production is 100 per cent higher.[23]

In India the Agriculture Department can decide that manure is most valuable when used as organic fertilizers for growing food then burned as a cooking fuel. Millions of tons over the next year can provide nutrients equal to the yearly volume of chemical fertilizers. In villages and fields in Mexico and Central America Peace Corp Volunteers from America and Russia without disrupting ancient ways can be assisting tribal farmers in modern techniques. The UN Food and Agricultural Organization can supply stronger oxen, aluminium plows, hybrid rice, new varieties of soy beans and a cross of wheat and rye which ultimately will lead to a doubling of the food supply in a decade. Irrigated lands will be planted with eight crops (Chart 14). The developing countries in Africa, South America and Asia total investment in the agricultural sector to 2000 amounts to nearly 1.5 trillion dollars.[24]

Thousand of years ago ancient mariners first invented boats and began to fish in the Mediterranean, Red Sea, Bay of Bengal and China Sea. As centuries passed, sails were added, vessels refined, distances extended and fish catches increased. During the 1600s, 1700s and 1800s coastal cities were living adequately off of the fish supply. However, the population was exploding at a tremendous rate pushing towards the limits of the planet.

The fishing industry in the 1900s on the east and west coast of the US and elsewhere began to move from wind power and wooden hull vessels to huge steel, motor driven, coal, wood and oil burning ships. By the 1950s, Japan was experiencing what the rest of the world would in two decades. The island's fisheries in the surrounding ocean were

FOOD—FEAST OR FAMINE

CHART 14

CROP PROJECTIONS 2000

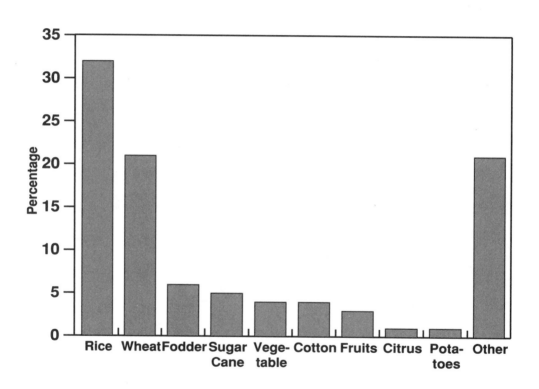

Source: "World Agriculture Toward 2000"
FAO

shrinking. In the 1980s overfishing had started and the per capita fish supply was declining globally (Chart 15).

If new UN fishing policies are not instituted then Tuna catches in the Pacific Ocean will continue to drop. In some ports in the US, Latin America and Canada fishermen and canneries will go out of business. Jobs and homes will be lost. If changes are not made immediately species of fish in the oceans will disappear and the food chain will be seriously disrupted.

In the future our global oceans should be used much like land; farmed for plants, harvested for fish, mined for minerals and the marine environment regulated for pollution. Effective management of the fisheries will avoid overfishing and provide larger catches in the short term, and a sustained yield during the coming century. Tropical fisheries around the Indonesian Islands and Caribbean need to be fully developed. Under the glacial ice of the North and South Pole in the 1990s special submarines can be fishing these abundant waters.

Converted Navy ships and fishing trawlers can be outfitted with sonar and precise computer data on individual species, their ranges and reproduction rate. In the Atlantic, Pacific, Indian, Arctic and Antarctic the fish will be caught within limits that allow the continuous replenishment of the schools. Multinationals, private companies and governments will need to put back what they take out by hatching and releasing fish near the surface where the oceans' life cycle takes place. Seaweed, kelp and plankton harvested by sailors can double adding a major new source of nutrients.

The projected increase in demand for direct human consumption of an additional 30 million tons of fish by the year 2000 might be satisfied by better fisheries management, 10 million tons, possible fish farm increases, 5 to 10 million tons, and improved utilization of resources, 15

FOOD—FEAST OR FAMINE

CHART 15

WORLD FISH CATCH
PROJECTIONS TO 2000

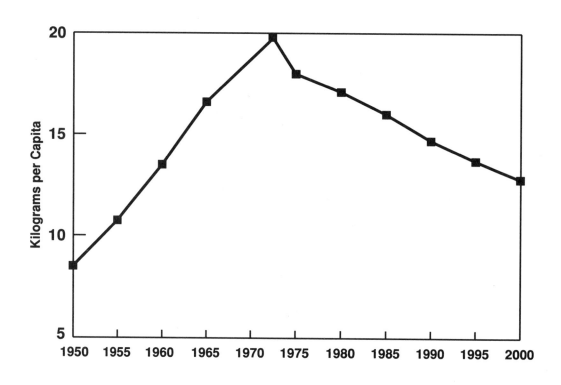

Source: Food and Agricultural Organization

to 20 million tons.[25] The world's aquaculture catch can rival agriculture in the production of food for the planet.

Water is an essential ingredient of all life today. It may well be the most precious resource the Earth provides to humankind. One might suppose that humans would be respectful of water, that they would seek to maintain its natural reservoirs and safeguard its purity. Yet people in countries throughout the world have been remarkably shortsighted and negligent. The future of the human species and many others are in jeopardy unless there is significant improvement in the management of the Earth's water resources.[26]

All the fresh water in the world's lakes, creeks, streams and rivers represents less than .01 per cent of the Earth's total store of water. Fortunately, this freshwater supply is continually replenished by the precipitation of rain or snow in the atmosphere. Unfortunately, much of that water vapor is contaminated on the way down by gases and particles that human activity introduces into the air. Fresh water runs off the land and on its way to the ocean becomes laden with dissolved matter, both natural and the wastes of human society. Waste matter in the water can be degraded by microbes through a process know as natural self-purification. However, when large quantities accumulate in the oceans, aquatic life is harmed.[27]

Because both the world's population and usable water are unevenly distributed, the local availability of water varies widely by country. The inhabitants of Bahrain have virtually no access to natural fresh water. They are dependent on the desalinization of seawater. The average US resident consumes more than 70 times as much water every year as a resident of Ghana. Although the uses to which water is put vary from country to country, agriculture is the main drain on the water supply. Averaged globally, 73 per cent of water withdrawn from the

Earth goes for that purpose. Depletion of groundwater is common in India, China, the US and Russia.[28]

The need for clean drinking water is becoming pressing because of the continuing rise in rural populations. Despite recent improvements, access to potable water has fallen. More than 1.5 billion people, roughly a third of the world's population primarily in underdeveloped countries, are without access.[29] The coverage in Europe for safe water is nearly 80 per cent[30], Russia less and the United States complete. However, industrialized nations in order to have safe drinking water need to eliminate the chemical and nuclear contaminants.

Local water shortages can be solved in two ways. The supply can be increased, either by damming rivers or by pumping groundwater. Or known supplies can be conserved, as by increasing the efficiency of irrigation. There is no doubt that water is becoming increasingly scarce as population, industry and agriculture all expand.[31]

Governments in Africa, Asia and South America will need to dig wells, install handpumps, invest in irrigation dams and commit themselves to maintaining healthy ground and surface water. Better access to potable water can be provided to all people regardless where they live or travel too.

Global starvation, malnutrition, inadequate food storage and lack of clean water effecting billions need not go on. Half measures will prove little more than a respite, a lull before a storm of crisis, even more damaging than what exists. Today, this can change in India, China, America, Russia and the world community. The US President and the Russian President have the power, leadership and wherewithal to do what is required. Accordingly, each nation has a check list of steps that need to be accomplished to solve food problems.

In a matter of weeks farming and fishing can be progressing on a

GLOBAL RENAISSANCE

five year timetable parallel with the disarmament and environment programs. This in turn will bring on a village, city and national Renaissance. Food shortages will no longer exist in any country including the forty poorest. In fact bumper crops and the promise of record harvests will be commonplace. All over supermarkets, groceries, restaurants, cafes, and homes will have plenty of healthy food. Parks, stadiums, recreation centers, hostels, camp sites and band shells will find people celebrating the new times.

CHAPTER 5

SUN, WIND AND
RENEWABLE FUELS

As we saw on television in the Persian Gulf War hundreds of oil fields were threatened and bombed. This is the lifeline from which about 68 per cent of Japan's, 32 per cent of Europe's[1] and 14 per cent of the United State's oil comes.[2] The multinational forces triumphed. UN Resolutions were complied with. However, world energy problems remain. A new oil crisis looms on the horizon.

Sooner than later motorists in New York to Los Angeles, Tokyo, Paris and London may again be sitting in their cars block after block in long gas lines. The cost per gallon or liter will begin to skyrocket at the pump. Rich and poor nations, industrial and Communist, alike, can be in the midst of an international oil crisis, as occurred in the 1970s and 1990. The gasoline, home heating oil and natural gas stored in the US, Russian and European cities range from days to three months.[3] If the energy crisis continues, congresses and parliaments will be called into all night emergency sessions. Fuel will have to be rationed. People will be jolted out of their daily routines. Cars will have to be left at home, mass transit will get overcrowded and behind schedule.

Coming when countries already are in the midst of a recession, a severe oil price rise will most likely cause millions of layoffs, result in higher food and fuel prices, force up inflation, cost Western Europeans, Americans, Russians and Japanese billions of additional dollars and lead to the collapse of many developing countries. These events will probably send the world into a depression.

If record blizzards strike this winter and there are extended subzero nights without home heating fuel. Then in American cities, as elsewhere millions probably will freeze to death or die of complications from pneumonia. Worldwide brutal cold temperatures will cause valves at nuclear reactors to malfunction and produce spontaneous explosions. Nuclear radiation will be spewed into the atmosphere, contaminating thousands of square miles, killing millions of people and infecting billions with radiation sickness and cancer.

Every twenty four hours the world produces and burns 60 million barrels of oil (Chart 16). This fuels the cities and operates the millions of vehicles on highways and waterways. The United States consumes annually 2.3 billion metric coal equivalent tons of energy, Russia and the commonwealth 1.9 billion, and Europe 2.2 billion.[4] Every year America to maintain the high standard of living burns 6.3 billion barrels of oil[5] for gasoline to power cars, trucks and planes, for fuel oils and gases to light and cool buildings and fire furnaces in plants. Humankind expends in 1 year an amount of fossil fuel that it took nature roughly a million years to produce.[6]

Even without an oil crisis large amounts of petrol are being pumped out of wells and more reserves are drying up. The dwindling petroleum supply cannot keep pace with the population explosion, food production, industrialization, and the demand for goods and products. The world commercial energy consumption has increased more than threefold over the past three decades.[7] In the US average crude oil productivity per well dropped from a peak level in 1972 to 13.4 barrels

CHART 16

WORLD DAILY CRUDE
OIL PRODUCTION

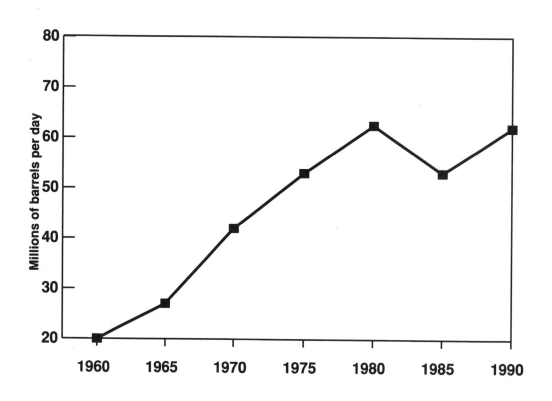

Source: US Department of Energy; Monthly Energy Review, 1991

per day in the late 1980s. Companies have been unable to sustain significant increases in production despite vast capital expenditures. In fact, these large investments merely enable companies to slow an inevitable production decline resulting from the predominance of old, heavily worked fields that characterize much of the US petroleum production base. The smaller number of producing wells, combined with declining productivity in many of the producing wells led to further declines in production.[8]

The world is desperately dependent on electricity supplies. Most nations are vulnerable to severe shortages. Serious problems confront the US to fuel its economy with electric power for the balance of the century. The situation is gloomy for the Third World, where economic expansion is forecast to grow at rates three to four times that of the United States. The projected demand for electrical power in Egypt, like other developing countries, will triple from 6,000 megawatts to 18,000 megawatts by the year 2000. A serious deficit in power generation capability can in turn act as a brake on economic development. In America if the annual growth rate in electric demand is as low as 1.4 per cent, the nation will need as much as 250,000 megawatts of new capacity in place by the year 2010. That is the equivalent of building 250 plants.[9]

The proved oil reserves, the pool of hyrdrocarbons, from which US companies can currently extract oil and gas constitute the domestic petroleum production stock. Energy forecasts indicate that there are 6 to 9 years of oil left in the dwindling underground US oil reserves.[10] World crude oil and natural gas reserves range from 20 to 40 years.[11] It becomes increasingly clear that the energy programs in place today in the United States, Russia and nearly all nations do not lead to global solutions but rather to a worsening day by day of living conditions, and growing international tension. If critical changes are not made, then all who are alive in the 21st century will be living in an energy dark age.

The US President can invite the Russian President to Camp David in the Maryland hills for a week of talks. There can be a news blackout. The statesmen, face to face, in a new spirit of cooperation can work out the difficulties and formulate an energy package explicitly designed to solve the global crisis.

In the months ahead the depression that is following in oils wake can diminish and turn into a prosperous Global Renaissance. The world is running out of oil, but not energy. Government policies, the international banking community and OPEC in conjunction with multinationals will largely determine what mix of fuels come on line and replace petroleum.

The energy sources will determine the kind and amount produced: in forested countries-wood; farming areas-methanol made from crops; rainy mountains-hydroelectric from new dams; along the ocean-tidal wave power; biomass in cities-out of garbage; breezy locales-windmills; in hot sunny climates-solar and futuristic technologies.

Moscow and Washington can arrange it, so the Russian and American people and others avoid the problems caused by a dwindling oil supply, and the transition goes smoothly to renewable, inexpensive, virtually endless energy.

Using former military space shuttles new satellites with solar panel wings nine miles long can be launched into synchronous orbit. One of these powersats can provide a portion of the total US output. The satellites are in sunlight all the time generating continuous electricity and will last for a hundred years. The energy can be beamed via microwave to a ground based antenna five miles in diameter.

Ocean thermal plants can be anchored off the coast of Indonesia, the United States, Japan, Taiwan and Cuba, steadily pushing 500 megawatts of electricity to shore. The energy source will be the sun. Warm water will be pumped down to a boiler, where its heat vaporizes a liquid. The gas drives the turbines.[12] These structures will take heat from the constantly flowing warm underwater gulf stream and drive low pressure turbines to generate electricity which will be relayed to shore by cable.

Wind power will be part of the future answer. Wherever the breezes are eleven to fourteen miles an hour energy can be produced. In the 1800s in Holland along the Zaan River was an industrial center. The windmills made it all go without the roar of engines and smoke. Europe, the Netherlands, Russia and other countries can double or triple wind power research and development.

Across America thousands of windmills are standing idle which can be fitted with new low cost turbines. Wind power can be commercial in most regions. In cities like Boston, New York, Chicago, Oklahoma City and San Francisco it can become widely used and popular (Chart 17). The quest for energy independence will spawn a variety of space age windmill designs. Home models can cost no more than a video recorder and generate free electricity.

Across Japan and China at strategic locales of high wind velocity super turbines using aerodynamic blades can whirl energy from the top of offices, schools and factories. Skyscrapers can mount large numbers of mini jets producing clean power.

The United Kingdom is making a major new commitment to build three wind farms, covering 750 to 1,000 acres apiece. The farms will each be equipped with 25 hundred foot high turbines putting out 300 to 500 kilowatts apiece.[13] Sweden is considering replacing its nuclear reactors with wind turbines anchored to the sea floor[14] In the North Sea an experimental turbine would have an output of 750 kilowatts and be mounted on a steel tripod sunk into the floor. Faster winds prevail

SUN, WIND AND RENEWABLE FUELS

CHART 17

WIND POWER

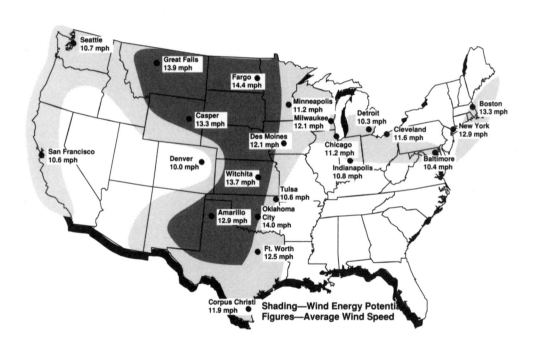

Source: National Geographic

offshore. An underwater cable will channel the electricity 3 miles back to land. Early next century the wind will give us economic electricity generation.[15]

The sun that shines on the Earth generates thousands of times more energy than is needed to meet the total daily demand in running cities and the transportation networks on all the continents. Harvesting the sunshine is clearly possible, and doing it economically in the 90s is a reality. For the first time solar energy can be captured worldwide with collectors, panels and photovoltaic cells producing electricity and heat at a low cost.

The day has come when solar cells can be delivered all over to houses like rolls of roofing paper, nailed on and plugged into the wiring, making the home its own power source. On the west coast of the US in Los Angeles, Phoenix and Las Vegas 80 to 90 per cent of the days are sunny.(Chart 18) The annual hours of sunshine across many countries are favorable for a flowering of solar technology.

Thousands of years ago the ancient Greeks, Romans and Chinese developed curved mirrors that concentrated the sun's rays onto an object and made it burst into flames. Solar mirrors captured people's imaginations for centuries. In the Renaissance in the 1500s there was a revival in solar technology among scientists and artists. But powerful burning mirrors proceeded slowly. In 1866 the first steam engine to run on energy from the sun was invented. In 1880 a solar-powered printing press was constructed. But the time wasn't right for solar energy. In Egypt in 1913 five solar collectors were built which pumped 6,000 gallons of water a minute for irrigation. In 1938 engineers at the Massachusetts Institute of Technology began two decades of research on the use of solar collectors for house heating. In 1954 researcher at Bell Laboratories made a discovery that revolutionized solar technology by inventing the silicon

SUN, WIND AND RENEWABLE FUELS

CHART 18

SOLAR ENERGY

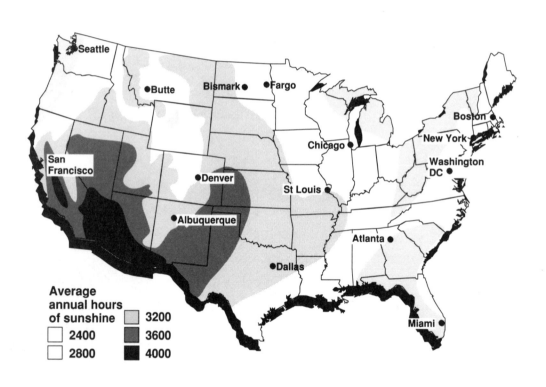

Average annual hours of sunshine

☐ 2400	▨ 3200
☐ 2800	▨ 3600
	■ 4000

Source: National Geographic

solar cell capable of producing a stable current from photons of light.[16] The solar age was dawning. In the 1960s and through the 90s the Americans and Russians advanced the technology by using photovoltaic cells on spacecraft.

Solar power generation is taking place on a large scale at plants that convert solar energy to heat. In these solar central thermal systems, mirrors or lenses focus sunlight onto a receiver containing a fluid that then conducts heat to an electric generator.[17]

In Italy and Ethopia thousands of heliostats covering square miles can be constructed. The mirrors mounted on a turntable and directed by a minicomputer will follow the sun, and reflect their soaring beams onto boosters at the top of 1,500 foot towers where steam generates electricity for use in metropolitan areas.

Villages in India can build and use new sun stoves and solar heaters which provide cheap hot water for the washing and bathing of families. Around the planet in deserts and sunbelts the sun's rays will produce most if not all of the energy.

At the bottom of the world at Antarctica new biosphere reserves with electric lodges can begin to go up on Weddell Sea along the Atlantic Ocean and Dumont Harbor on the Indian Ocean. The nearby glacier ice can be used as a vast source of energy. New fusion plants might be constructed which separate the hydrogen in the melted water from the oxygen and provide endless, clean, renewable fuel. People from all over can explore this virgin continent and its wildlife sanctuaries. The abundance of energy and the rich diversity of cultures will in time produce a unique Antarctica civilization.

In Africa on the Congo River six nations in a consortium can erect a series of modern dams. Engineers and construction workers will come from surrounding villages. At the same time on the Orineo River in

SUN, WIND AND RENEWABLE FUELS

South America Venezuela, Columbia and Brazil can plan and construct hydroelectric stations. The energy generated by the turbines can become a substantial percentage of the power for the regions. Modern oasis cities will come to life along the rivers on both continents.

Los Angeles, Tokyo, Rotterdam, Capetown and other coastal metropolis can harness the power of the tides. Shoreline generation stations can be installed using the flow and ebb of the water through micromotors to generate electricity. The American tides run approximately 2 to 32 feet, African 7 to 23 feet, European 3 to 30 feet, South American 1 to 41 feet, and Asian 2 to 30 feet.[18] In the morning and evening at high and low tide during peak traffic the net of underwater generators will be on, and the cost of energy for the express trains and electric cars will be very inexpensive. Millions of workers can find new jobs in the construction and installation of these huge projects.

In Boston, Moscow, Paris, Peking and elsewhere garbage, waste paper and sewage can be converted to methane gas yielding additional energy. New high-tech recycling facilities will be added to treatment plants. Robot operated machinery will convert underwater sludge in canals and rivers to methane producing extra energy besides ridding the environment of pollutants.

In California's High Sierra mountains engineers are boring a 20,000 foot hole. Scientists believe that molten reservoirs within six miles of the surface contain up to a half million quads of energy. Annual American energy consumption is about 80 quads. Many years of energy are stored in the magma. Computer analysis of the wave patterns suggests that chambers are oozing magma just four to six miles below the surface. Heat can be extracted from the molten rock using a heat exchange device. Cool liquid is pumped down a casing of the well hole for conversions into steam in the magma reservoir. It would return to the surface in an insulated pipe at the center of the casing.[19] Renewable methane is interchangeable with the dwindling non-renewable natural gas. Their main burnable component is the same. Methane can be pumped for storage into underground formations that once held oil and gas.

Agricultural expansion can yield efficient and massive amounts of fuel. This spring farmers in America like those in Brazil and Australia can plant fallow land in sugarcane, corn, potatoes and grain. Portable distillation plants can be flown into fields by helicopters. The crops will be harvested and methanol distilled and stored. This fuel in turn can replace gasoline and coal. Tall grasses, reeds and fast growing shrubs, as well as manure, can also be turned into methanol.

In Iceland and New Zealand old and new cities built near hot water geysers will use the steam that naturally comes up from the earth to heat homes and generate electricity. Electric trams on the cobblestone streets and futuristic houses can be operating off of geothermal energy.

Coal, although plentiful in some countries, will no longer be competitive. Due to the high cost of pollution abatement equipment and the tax on pollutant emission coal won't be profitable to companies. The enormous cost overruns on the construction of nuclear plants, the disasters and the dangers of the radiation waste will cause this source to be phased out.

Promoting energy efficiency is relatively painless. The US reduced the energy intensity of its domestic product by 23 per cent between a recent 12 year period without much notice. Substantial improvement in efficiency is available with existing technology. Something as simple as bringing all US buildings up to the best world standards can save enormous amounts of energy. Right now more energy passes through the windows of buildings in the US than flows through the Alaska pipeline.

SUN, WIND AND RENEWABLE FUELS

By adhering to the US Appliance Standards will save 28 billion dollars in energy costs by the year 2000 and keep 342 million tons of carbon out of the atmosphere. Compact fluorescent lamps can replace incandescent bulbs and window coating and save energy during both heating and cooling seasons. At current rates of implementation, the new technologies can generate 63 billion dollars in energy savings by the year 2010.[20]

In India a 1 million dollar factory could produce enough fluorescent light bulbs to save the country 204 billion dollars annually by not having to build additional power plants.[21] The municipal solid waste produced in the U.S. including garbage and biomass contains materials with an energy equivalent of over 500 million barrels of oil a year.[22] New power plants can be built utilizing this fuel. Similar innovations and adaptations in other industrialized and developing countries will have a substantial effect in saving energy.

Solar automobiles with photovoltaic cells on the roof and body can be manufactured on all the continents in the factories currently producing gas operated vehicles. The assembly lines can be reworked. The technology in at hand. In the 1,867 mile World Solar Challenge race across Australia[23] the winning car's top speed was 50 mph. Engineers in auto firms can readjust future models and put out stylish, safe, inexpensive, non-polluting, solar vehicles.

In the US nine of the ten largest photovoltaic companies are owned by multinational corporations. 99 per cent of domestic copper production, essential for making solar heating equipment, is owned or controlled by the oil industry.[24] In Russia a few men control the energy future, as with Europe and most nations. Without much difficulty petroleum can be phased out and renewable energies phased in.

The manufacturing of battery operated cars, vans and trucks can be expanded substantially by the auto industry or through government incentives. In 1990 General Motors Corporation unveiled an advanced electric passenger car that has a top speed of 75 m.p.h. and can accelerate from 0 to 60 in 8 seconds. The aerodynamic Impact can go 124 miles on a single charge and even outrace gas cars. It is powered by 32 10 volt lead-acid batteries and uses about a third of the energy of a conventional auto. The electricity to run the electric car will cost 5 to 12 dollars a month. Expected improvements in battery design in the next three to four years can extend battery life to 50,000 miles. Eventually recharging circuits will be placed around cities, much as some Canadian cities put outlets at parking meters. The advanced electric cars will result in pollution reductions of up to 90 per cent. GM plans to go into production for the consumer market in 1993 or 1994. Chrysler and Ford Motor Company are also developing their own electric powered vehicles.[25] America's current offpeak capacity would be sufficient to accommodate nearly 20 million electric cars.[26]

Engineers at West Germany's Daimler-Benz AG have developed new engines for cars like the Mercedes that run on hydrogen. They emit almost nothing but steam, no carbon dioxide to heat the planet and no exhaust to endanger the forests. Producing the fuel involves a process of extracting hydrogen from water.[27]

The oil and gas fuels can be replaced with an abundance of ethanol and methane which can be used in pollution free internal combustion engines with heat exchangers. Manufacturers can produce prototype cars that obtain nearly 100 miles to the gallon.[28]

Atmospheric carbon dioxide may be converted to methanol and used as a fuel for futuristic cars. Chemists have developed specialized molecules than can remove CO_2 from the air which is then reduced electrochemically to carbon monoxide and then to methanol for fuel.[29] On superhighways and autobahns electronic fibers can be installed enabling cars to hook onto a beam. Drivers will then switch to automatic, sit back and enjoy the trip.

Where the US and Russia border, at ıne Bering Strait, a 30 mile underwater energy cable can be laid. The superpower Presidents and the rest of the world might see on television live underwater video of American and Russian aquanauts swim out of submarines and connect a high tech energy cable on the ocean floor. In the White House and Kremlin the leaders can push a remote control device and the massive electrical grids of the superpowers will be connected. The surplus energy generated during the day in the United States or Russia will then be transmitted through the cable for use by the other at night.

If five years ago in America, Russia, Europe, Japan and other countries the governments, banks, multinationals, and utility companies, had initiated the available energy innovations, then today people would be reaping the benefits with an abundance of renewable fuels, and hundreds of billions of dollars in savings.

America, as well as the world, in the past 150 years has changed its source of energy two times. First it switched from wood to coal during the mid 1800s. Trees taking decades to grow were being burned for fuel in a matter of minutes. In the early 1900s the economy switched from coal to petroleum (Chart 19).

The 1990s have brought about a general realization that fossil fuels are finite and that countries should use other sources and establish an appropriate energy mix to meet the demands for sustainable development.

Projections of energy demand in the world vary from 9.5 billion t.o.e. to 12 billion t.o.e. by the year 2000.[30] It is quite apparent that with the oil crisis and petrol reserves running out, humankind will be living in the post petroleum era in a matter of years.

GLOBAL RENAISSANCE

CHART 19

FUELS IN THE
UNITED STATES

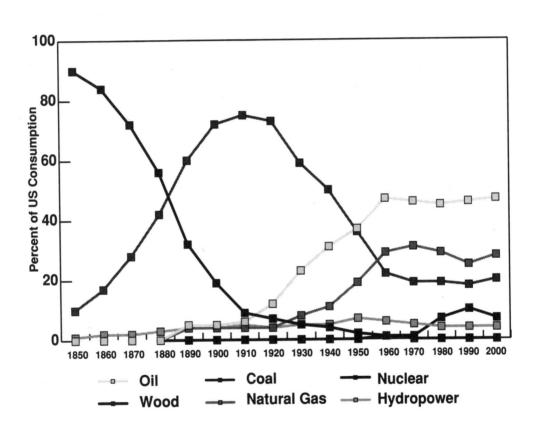

Source: US Department of Energy

SUN, WIND AND RENEWABLE FUELS

Industrial and centrally planned economies, the United States, Russia, the commonwealth and Europe, account for 66 per cent of the total global consumption of commercial energy.[31] Clearly, the US and Russian Presidents and the President of the European Community can via three way television, arrange things to happen, take bold energy actions and be partners in changing the world.

There is no reason for an oil crisis, nuclear plant explosions, long gas lines, brown outs in the summer, white outs in the winter, worsening conditions and unnecessary deaths to be part of the future. The risk to humanity, the waste of natural resources and the endangerment of the planet is too great for the superpowers to continue to delay.

The global energy transformation can begin this week. A dramatic turn of events can take place in Moscow, Washington and other capitols. The superpower presidents and the handful of men who run the other nations can take the needed steps and phase in long overdue energy programs.

The leaders can shut down in a matter of weeks the nuclear power industries. An emergency radioactive waste disposal operation will need to immediately go into effect. Scientists will be connected via TV, computers and fax, and come up with breakthroughs in the elimination of nuclear radiation hazards. National and intercontinental energy grids will be connected to boost the energy transition.

Inside city and congressional halls officials can pass legislation which allows corporations, businesses and home owners credit and subsidies for renewable energy installations. New bills will initiate conservation and authorize governments to install photovoltaic cells, which will lead to the rapid commercialization of solar devices. Individuals will need to conserve energy, insulate, buy energy efficient automobiles, appliances and lighting.

GLOBAL RENAISSANCE

Most informed people agree when these actions are taken the world will be awash in endless, clean, cheap energy. In turn this will boost development and prosperity in the Americas, Europe, Asia and Africa in the next five years and bring on a golden age.

CHAPTER 6

CITIES AND CIVILIZATION
IN THE 21ST CENTURY

A spaceship will return home to Earth from a historic journey to Mars. The American Astronauts and Russian Cosmonauts will pass orbiting satellites which monitor global weather, pollution and harvests. People can be living in their own homes in cities and on farms. Housing renewal can be in full bloom all over the planet. Two mile glass skyscrapers, subterranean cities and orbiting space colonies can be under construction.

However, today living conditions around the globe are in a crisis state. Access to decent shelter has worsened for increasing segments of the population in most countries. The deteriorating housing situation is too critical to leave unattended.

In the United States 660 thousand to 3 million people are homeless.[1] 1.5 million are lacking some or all plumbing. 32 per cent of the people rent their residences.[2] There is little doubt that home buyers are suffering with mortgage rates and too few home loans.

Russia and Eastern Europe regard decent housing to be a basic right to be enjoyed by all citizens. However, housing is considered to be one of the most pressing of social problems. In Russia the amount of city houses not equipped with a fixed lavatory is 11 per cent.[3]

GLOBAL RENAISSANCE

All centrally planned countries are trailing in the construction of new dwelling units as compared to the households formed. Production fell by 7 per cent in ten years. The situation is more critical when the waiting lists for scarce state supplied residences and co-operative units are taken into account. The wait for an apartment is likely to range from 5 years in Czechoslovakia, 4 to 10 years in Hungary and 15 to 30 years in Poland.[4]

The slums in London, Stockholm, Rome and other Western European cities are where rundown old tenement buildings and the density of people are some of the worst. Millions survive in decrepit squalor. Rural areas in many countries are still without adequate plumbing.

In China the population's typical living condition consist of one or two rooms per family with a communal kitchen and bathroom. Of China's urban housing stock 66 per cent have no toilets.[5] There are no private homes. A severe housing shortage exists. In the crowded streets of Bombay and Calcutta 400,000 people are living and sleeping.[6] Millions of street people subsist without shelters in many other cities throughout India.

In the developing countries of Africa, Asia and South America 40 to 50 per cent of the inhabitants are living in slums and informal settlements. In Rio, Cairo, Caracas and elsewhere on the side of hills in squatter camps millions of peasants live in cardboard make shift huts. Sanitation conditions are unhealthy. The death toll is high, especially among the children. In Mexico City, nearly one third of all families sleep in a single room and 40 per cent have no or very inadequate sanitation.[7]

Presently in the Republic of Korea 46 per cent of households in large urban areas share the same small crowded dwelling with other families.[8] Japan has an acute shortage of inexpensive rental accommodations in some large cities, but to date little has been done to alleviate it.[9]

In the Third World near garbage dumps and in shanty towns in Manila, Sao Paulo, Nairobi and Ankara millions needlessly live in hovels and mud shacks.[10] In refugee camps in Thailand, Pakistan, Iran, Sudan, Honduras and at 90 other refugee sites, 15 million people of all ages are sleeping in tents or outside and require immediate housing.[11]

Clearly, 1 billion people are in dire need of adequate dwellings.[12] Throughout most of the world the home building industry is in a depression. Housing starts in the US compared to a few years ago are down 30 per cent[13] as in Europe and other countries.

The uncomfortable truth is the global housing crisis is getting worse everyday, because the present policies are outdated and out of step with reality. Nearly every city faces the same problem. Building has failed to keep pace with the rapid population explosion. No one can call the attempts at housing by the United States, Russia, China and India a solution.

The limited approaches will not lead to success. The old failures should not be part of the future. Civilization need not descend to chaos for the unique opportunity to rebuild the cities of our beautiful planet. The global problems need not extend another month, continue into next year, or escalate into the ensuing century.

The US President, the Russian President and all other leaders can no longer turn their backs on the poor living conditions and poverty. Especially since these can be remedied in a matter of years. The superpower presidents, regardless of other obligations, must take the time, even if it is daily two-way television meetings, to solve our common global problems. The statesmen can formulate a comprehensive long term housing plan.

GLOBAL RENAISSANCE

Currently the US, Russia and other central government expenditures for housing are in the range of 2 to 4 per cent [14] whereas defense is 6 to 18 per cent.[15] Today, the American and Russian Presidents can come on television and announce to the world community that a historic turning point had been reached. The trillion dollars that is scheduled for the military, a percentage would be reallocated into new housing programs. The great powers can undertake their global destines, set in motion the necessary national programs and overcome the initial international resistance.

Capitalist, Socialist and Communist strategies can enable substantially more people to be adequately housed and help foster economic growth in a changing global economy. Commitments to new housing enterprises will rejuvenate the building industry creating a strong demand for homes. It will facilitate people's access to decent and affordable housing. This will help lift all economies out of the current depression and into a recovery.

By tapping entrepreneurship, savings, private property, local building materials, cost effectiveness, the unemployed and other underutilized resources the supply of housing can expand and improve substantially. Loans and grants can be made available from lending institutions and the United Nations model cities programs. These approaches will make it possible for Renaissance living to emerge in the weeks ahead and continue into the coming century.

In the United States nearly 9 million housing units are vacant[16], boarded up and abandoned in cities from New York to San Francisco. Rather than being demolished in a few hours these houses, apartments, tenements and factories can be in a few months fixed up and renovated into new homes, condos and electronic cottages for millions of people. Bold national approaches to housing finance can be undertaken by congress, the banking community, the Federal Reserve and the Treasury Department.

In ghettos and barrios people can be trained with skills to remodel their own homes. Neighborhood renewal programs will bring back to life clusters of old houses around city squares and parks. Homesteading and gentrification will become widespread. As a result poverty will drop and property values go up. Living will flourish in a new way throughout America.

Leading US airplane manufacturers in Seattle, Houston and Los Angeles can put together on their assembly lines new energy efficient aircraft, mini helicopters and jet backpacks. Some of the factories can be retooled to produced new types of electronic mini-homes. These will be rolled from the factory, jet vertical wings mounted, flown all over, landed and serve as homes for futuristic towns of 5,000 to 15,000. The modern dwellings equipped with voice activated computers and artificial intelligence will allow people to stay home to work, rather than spend hours on the freeway commuting. Along the coast of Boston, Florida, San Diego and Alaska entertainment marinas can be constructed with 200 channel satellite dishes and hydrofoil jet boats.

The cities of the future in America will build on their own unique characteristics, as represented by their historic downtowns. Changes will be dramatic with advances in telecommunications. Modern offices will increasingly provide day care, gyms and training centers. Cities will undertake major downtown forestry programs, with thousands of new trees planted along streets and parks.[17] Twenty-two cities are planning to expand or build new aquariums. Arts and education will increase.[18]

The average size of a residential lot in the United States peaked in the late 1970s at 1,879 square meters, signaling the beginning of a slow contraction in lot size. Individual yards may give way to common space to reduce land costs. Village Homes, a 200 household development in California, is built in clusters of 8 to 10 homes with no front lawns and shared backyards. The acreage is maintained by the community and includes vegetable gardens, fruit trees and playing areas.[19]

Personal rapid transit, small vehicles operating under remote control on guideways, will extend throughout metropolitan areas. Miami and Detroit currently have experimental systems. By the year 2000 virtually all waterfront cities will have reclaimed much of their downtown shorelines for public access and mixed-use development. Increased nationwide hostel programs will provide travel accommodations for young people who want to see America.[20]

A new reality in housing must be mirrored in all nations. In Russia and the commonwealth the autonomy for construction enterprises, the payment of bonuses and performance controls that encourage early completion of works and penalize delays, can be implemented. Housing projects involving the use of private construction brigades working on a profit basis can produce encouraging results.[21] When the new leaders in the independent states give direction and guidance to housing plans great changes will take place over a short period of time.

Across Russia 2 million dwellings are annually constructed.[22] The numbers can be doubled or tripled raising the total housing stock substantially by the 2000s. The Army can be put to work building rather than destroying. Throughout Moscow and St. Petersburg millions of people can be moving into privately owned homes and apartments. At the same time there can develop luxurious hotels and five star restaurants. Cities will have a great period of revitalization with new parks, plazas, open spaces, sculpture and water fountains. In Kiev major performing arts centers and sports arenas will need to be built. Classic old music halls and movie palaces will be renovated. A new wave of art districts will spring up near famous museums. The lands along the rivers in Russia, Ukraine, Belarus and Kazakhstan will need to be protected as national parks for generations to come.

In the new Europe Bulgaria can place sharp restrictions on the construction of multi storey blocks of flats and instead stress the building of low-storey residential dwellings. In Hungary do it yourself housing construction can be greatly facilitated by a plentiful supply of domestically produced building materials. As a result, the housing can increase significantly.[23]

Investment by the ministries of the Eastern European Nations in express trains, highway systems and electric trolleys can increase travel. An automobile revolution can sweep Russia with one car per family the standard. Construction of youth hostels and overnight dachas with kitchenettes will naturally increase. Conversion of military plants to consumer goods will accelerate. Pollution free factories will be built, and expand the production of television, telephones, refrigerators and computers. People and business alike will prosper. Modern homes and human rights will be popular all over.

Urban renewal throughout Western Europe as in Italy must be of national concern. The historic inner city cores can be spared from the bulldozers. Town-planners interested in the preservation of the architecture will supervise. Italian inner city housing solutions can led to a wide range of citizen initiatives modeled on the principle of self-help. Numerous successful community renovation programs can be duplicated in neighborhoods. Shortly housing will be heading in a new direction.[24] The United Kingdom can revitalize London, Liverpool and other inner cites with new policy measures designed to reverse the crisis and build the types of houses people want. It's goals should be to improve the physical fabric of cities and to make the environment attractive for housing. Those areas most urgently in need will be targeted as enterprise zones. Revitalization will take place. When new legislation is implemented it will achieve promising results.[25] Spain to Sweden, Ireland to Germany will combat the decline in livable dwellings by setting housing as a top priority. Millions of families will move into new homes near amphitheaters and amusement parks. Castles can be turned into condominiums. Eventually utopian cities will come about.

The years of warfare need no longer drain China of people's lives and scarce resources. In the months to come the army can be dismantled and city construction progress. As the old in power pass, new leaders with new thinking will take the reigns. A monumental nationwide housing program can get underway immediately. Hundreds of millions of private bungalows and terraced farms can be built. Inevitably, civil liberties, a free press, multi-party elections and democracy will be widespread and part of modern China.

China's long range plans call for constructing an apartment for every urban household on the basis of 8 sq. meters of floor space per person and 100 for each family by the year 2000. This ambitious program will require an enormous increase in construction during the period. For urban housing alone it will require a doubling of the current annual use of 27.5 million tons of steel, 71 million tons of cement, 39 million cubic meters of lumber, 220 million bricks and 32 million standard cases of glass.[26]

The Chinese government projects that by next century there can be a 10 fold increase in foreign tourists visiting the country each year. A large scale hotel building and renovation program is underway in the major tourist centers.[27] Billions will be spent for the construction of new railways and passenger trains. China plans to expand its extensive highway system. A massive airport upgrading and rebuilding program to meet sharply higher air traffic service are set for the next 5 years.[28]

Archaeological parks in Peking can be constructed near thousands of year old ruins with new museums, opulent hotels and forest camp sites. Artisans will need to be recruited to carry on the exacting work of restoring these ancient structures. In the years to come China will blend the old with the new in the Chinese Renaissance.

In India rather than being in financial ruin, deeply in debt and unable to meet the 800 million Indians housing needs, eventually the parliament will decide not to spend money on outdated military equipment. Instead funds will be channeled into simple flats, low cost homes and artistic civic centers.

Civilian mobs, riots and political disarray will no longer bring down the Indian governments. The prime minister can develop programs to deal effectively with the serious housing crisis. People will no longer needlessly suffer. Government lands can be opened for new homesteads. Bombay, Delhi and other cities that have known greatness and splendor will once again be in blossom. The infrastructure water supply, roads, sanitation system and bridges will need to be improved. Huge sports stadiums, entertainment complexes and botanical gardens can be constructed near harbors. Society and religion once again will uplift the human spirit.

In Bangkok, Thailand developers can move downmarket and build small two storey terraced housing units on individually owned plots on the periphery of the city. Because of the reduced construction costs and easy access to mortgage financing over 20 years, the dwellings could be affordable to 60 per cent of the urban population.[29]

In the Australian State of Victoria 500 elder cottages are being lived in by grandparents. Here and elsewhere pre-built units provide low cost alternative housing. These relocatable homes for aging parents are placed in the backyards of their children which eases the strains on isolated nuclear families.[30]

Turkey can expand the General Housing Fund which derives it's capital from an excise tax on petroleum products, luxury imports, trips, tobacco and alcohol. The fund would lend money to help finance another 350,000 dwelling units.[31]

Japan is currently the world leader in the production of prefabricated housing and should retain that role through the next decade.[32] A plug in tower has already been constructed and is marketing models through a Tokyo department store. The structure consists of a central core for support and the removable capsules. A crane attaches the living unit to the central tower which contains elevators and service facilities. People will someday buy capsules and take them from city to city as they move.[33] Prefab wood housing units, modules and panelization, are expected to increase their share of the housing market by the year 2000.[34]

Home remodeling in Japan, as in other countries, will continue to be seen as an effective, less costly means to improve the condition of a dwelling. The Ministry of Construction will make 7,400 acres of land in the Tokyo area available for residential use over the next 10 years which can accommodate some 15,000 building lots. This can inject some needed life into the Tokyo housing market.[35]

Japan can stimulate its economy through housing construction and public works investment. Two generation term mortgages can again prove successful in setting off a wave of demand and housing construction starts.[36] The inherent technical ingenuity of the Japanese can be reflected in Osaka neighborhoods with high-tech cottages, plastic flats and pagoda duplexes with hot tubs and holigraphic TV. Ginza street will be crowded with international travelers. City parks will open out into new tea gardens which in turn merge with simple retreat lodges.

In Puerto Rico hexagonal units with private terraces have been stacked in various ways to create large communities on mountain slopes. The single modules, with the walls serving both as structural supports and space dividers, are aggregated in a variety of ways to create large modular systems. Since modules can be mass produced in factories, it offers a way to house people that is less expensive than traditional methods.[37]

Despite the difficulties South America can make profound changes, transfer the corps of engineers and provide former army bulldozers, trucks and helicopters to the housing ministries. The slums without water, the barrios with raw sewage, the villages without clinics that exist will need to be fixed. People will get involved in local self help housing projects. Pipes will need to be laid in Columbia, Venezuela, Peru and Brazil. For a small per capita investment the walls and roofs to simple houses can go up and families start gardens. Millions of homesteads and plots of land in agrarian reform projects can be made available to compesinos willing to settle and clear the land in Nicaragua, Argentina and Mexico. Along the Amazon and other rivers, towns will be renovated into splendid cities with flowered streets, restored old buildings and tree lined haciendas.

In the decades ahead, architects and homebuilders in industrialized and agrarian countries will have at their disposal a wide variety of new materials and techniques that will free them to create buildings dramatically different from those known in the past. New electronic technology will greatly change homes and homelife. Precast sections of fiberglass can be connected by flexible corridors to permit many design variations. Lightweight and movable, the structures fold up like an umbrella for transportation, or are laid out in all sorts of shapes to meet specific needs.[38]

GLOBAL RENAISSANCE

Urethane can be sprayed on a variety of molds to create exciting structures and interior spaces. After the recent earthquake disaster in Turkey, a reusable inflatable plastic mold was sprayed with foam to provide instant shelter for the homeless. Based on aerospace technology is the filament wound system. It involves the wrapping of continuous strands of resin-coated glass filaments around a collapsible mold to produce on site housing shells. This makes it possible for the architect to sculpt buildings according to almost any design.[39]

Africa once again can rival its great past. Ancient cities rather than left rundown and unhealthy can be restored, and squares and old buildings preserved. Exquisite shops, coffee houses and cabarets will expand. The commercial districts will be surrounded by wide boulevards. Local tribes at huge wildlife game reserves with elephants, rhinos and giraffes can build nature lodges with water and solar energy. The booming African housing sector will increase its stocks by millions of dwellings a year. New schools, technical colleges, teaching hospitals and universities in Nigeria, Ethiopia, Kenya, South Africa, like elsewhere, connected to global libraries via telecommunication, will be constructed.

In the future more buildings will be built under the Earth. Houses, offices and factories can be built underground to ease the increasing congestion of the surface areas. The dirt provides good insulation not only from heat and cold but noise as well. Underground structures are nothing new. Prehistoric people lived in caves. Ancient Egypt had temples in caves. Early Christians held services in the catacombs of Rome.[40]

In Nice, France and Vail, Colorado earth sheltered buildings are burrowed into hillsides too steep for conventional housing. They merge into the landscape, do not obstruct the view and leave more space for gardens or lawns. Ten homes per acre can be built on otherwise hard to use land.[41]

Sweden has constructed the world's most comprehensive underground facilites in the form of a giant naval base inside the rocks of Musko near Stockholm. Among the subterranean facilites are offices, complete airplane factories, hangars for jet aircraft and a hospital with 1,600 beds.[42] In a year this facility can be converted into a modern resort with gardens.

The city of Montreal has attractive underground shops, offices, restaurants, cinemas and pedestrian walkways. All of which are safely away from the worst Canadian blizzards. New underground facilities require three times less heat, 10 times less refrigeration and 15 times less operating cost providing a dramatic savings in fuel costs. Day or night, summer or winter, from the frigid north to the tropics, whatever the air temperature, a few feet below the ground it remains fairly constant. Underground buildings require a small amount of energy.[43]

With seven tenths of the Earth's surface covered by oceans, marine structures offer one possible answer to the urban crisis. Stemming from the twin pressures of Tokyo's population explosion and scarcity of land, the Tokyo Bay project has developed many ways to use the bay for residential and commercial purposes. The marine structures are either floating or stationary. Stable structures are usually built on pylons similar to those used on offshore drilling platforms. Bridge structures housing people are constructed of girder or cable systems stretching between tower supports. Aquapolis floats at anchor off the Japanese coast near Okinawa. It now offers housing that cost less than the typical rent in Tokyo.[44]

Floating cities with concrete pontoons as flotation platforms can soar 2,740 meters above the sea and contain one million people. Sea City is a floating megastructure proposal developed in England. Built on shoals 24 kilometers from the coast of Norfolk, this city can be an offshore island for 30,000 inhabitants. Piles and floating concrete pontoons will support the 16 story structure. Apartments and recreational facilities will fill its upper decks with industry contained in the lower areas.[45]

Increasing population densities on land may provide a major impetus for moving underwater in some coastal areas. The undersea living and research environments now used by scientists and drilling teams foreshadow the development of subsurface communities. Researchers have already established permanent undersea habitats off the coast of Texas, Florida and the Grand Bahamas. Newly developed gas mixtures and improved decompression techniques for surviving underwater are becoming more numerous and refined. Undersea structures will facilitate research in marine biology as well as provide vacationers with an exciting locale. Large ocean resorts made up of chambered undersea houses anchored to the floor can be constructed in the next decade.[46]

Paralleling these developments at the North and South Pole huge craters 500 feet deep and miles long can be dug. Large prefabricated geodesic domes can be airlifted with former military helicopters and set up. Top soil may be brought in, fields and trees planted, laser heaters installed and the temperature maintained. People can then settle in newly built subterranean structures with parks, animals and malls.

Third world cities stand at the crossroads as the population swells and urban transportation rapidly multiplies. To meet the mobility needs of the poor majority substantial improvements and expansion of public transport are required. Electric trolleys and cheap light-rail systems are now a favored option. In Asia buses, streetcars, human powered rickshaws, pedicabs, pushcarts and animal drawn wagons can be improved and made more efficient.[47]

In large African cities like Kinshasa walking accounts for two thirds of all trips and for almost half in Bangalore, India. The overwhelming majority of travel in China's cities are made by bike, as in many developing nations. In the future bicycles will be integrated with cars and mass transit. This will help save energy and other resources, reduce pollution and provide mobility to people. Outstanding models of nationwide bicycle plans are in the Netherlands, West Germany and Japan. The Netherlands has over 9,000 miles of bicycle paths. Japanese commuters ride their bikes to train stations. In the United States nearly 2 million people commute which represents a quadrupling in one decade. Around the world more than 100 million bicycles are made each year, three times the automobiles.[48] In the 1990s around the globe automated modern factories can be constructed. Massive numbers of nonpolluting vehicles will come off the assembly lines to meet the needs of an emerging middle class.

At the Bering Strait Wilderness Park in a joint venture by the US and Russia thirty miles of key bridges, an island resort with geodesic domes and international hotels, can be constructed. The space-tech structure may be decorated with flags. The US President and the Russian President may land there in a jetcopter for a ribbon cutting ceremony commemorating a new Peace Bridge. Eventually the 400 mph monorail trains linking Moscow and Los Angeles will depart on their maiden trips.

Stratophonic planes carrying 1,000 travelers and semi-orbital flights to any place on our planet in 45 minutes can open up a new continental lifestyle. People can live in one country and commute to another. Huge music festivals in the Americas, Europe, Asia and Africa will draw fans from all over in solar and electric cars.

GLOBAL RENAISSANCE

At the turn of the century 300 miles overhead the space station Freedom, constructed by the US, Canada, Japan and Europe, a permanent outpost in space, can be completed. It will be more than 500 feet long, contain four modules for living and working and have the capability to add more. Space walking astronauts for two years will link girders, solar panels and electronic equipment in a space home.[49]

From the dark days in the 1990s of the international recession, unemployment, inflation, bank failures and factory closings, with statesmanship an economic miracle can awaken the world. The American and Russian economies, particularly, will be up and rolling. Homes, urban renovation, cities and monumental building projects will be a major priority for all nations. Hundreds of millions of jobs are required. When societies' potentials are mobilized the UN goal of housing for all before the year 2000 will become a reality.

However, unless our human family is educated, ten thousand years of civilization will not last long. In the global age learning is the key to survival and a good life. Unfortunately, today universal education is not common place around our planet.

The number of the population aged 15 years and above who are illiterate increased to 825 million in the developing countries. The highest is in Africa with 60 percent, Asia and the Pacific 40 per cent and Latin America 20 per cent.[50] The gap between males and females is substantial. The adult illiteracy rate in Bangladesh was male 57 per cent, female 78 per cent, India 43 per cent and 71 per cent, Nepal 61 per cent and 88 per cent.[51]

In industrial and developing countries education subsidies are much greater for higher than lower institutions, particularly in Africa. Accordingly, the largest number of students receive a disproportionately low subsidization. The very small percentage of the population able to

CHART 20

**COST OF
PUBLIC EDUCATION**

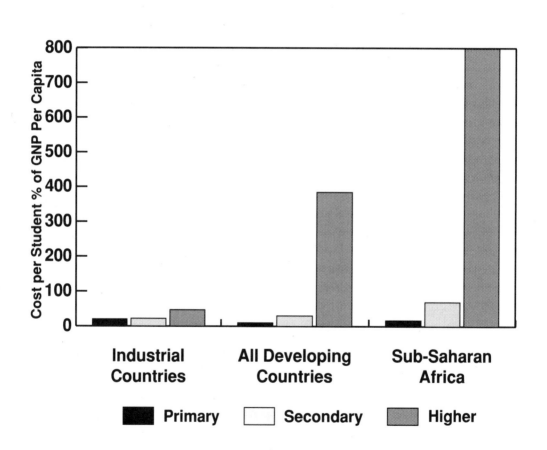

Source: World Bank

gain access to higher education receives a larger share of the education budget.[52] This contributes directly to illiteracy (Chart 20).

Six countries in the Eastern Mediterranean have already reached the goal of 70 per cent adult literacy. In Sri Lanka and Thailand the overall figure rose to 90 per cent. In Europe the adult lliteracy rates are above 95 per cent except in four countries. In the United States and Russia nearly all people are educated.[53]

However, Russian and European, like American schools are failing many students. American eighth graders taking standardized math tests answered only 46 per cent of the questions correctly, which put them in the bottom half of the 11 nations participating. The top 5 per cent of twelfth graders from nine developed countries, who had taken advanced math courses, took standardized tests of algebra and calculus. American students' came in last. In the US more than 500,000 children drop out of school each year.[54] 26 per cent don't graduate and less than 20 per cent earn a college degree.[55]

The US Federal government is spending after inflation about 14 per cent less for education than it did five years ago.[56] In sub Saharan Africa, due to the poor economic conditions, real expenditure for each pupil in primary education declined in 17 out of the 25 low income countries.[57]

Widespread unemployment among young people today in both developed and developing countries emphasizes the need for education to be relevant to social and economic conditions.[58] Education affects health, fertility and life. Educated farmers are 10 per cent more productive than those with no education. 30 per cent of GDP growth can be ascribed to education. The most cost effective educational investments must be determined on a country by country basis.[59] However, to bring the enrollment up in developing countries to the average achieved in the developed will mean that an additional 230 million of today's school age population enroll. The annual cost of this expansion will be less than 50 billion dollars, one third of the 150 billion a year that developing countries are now spending on the arms race.[60]

The challenge of school systems and educators in all nations is to meet the new demands of people for our modern times. There is a need for more global education about the world, its problems and solutions, interdependencies, international institutions and the future.

It is the self-enlightened interest of governments to educate their children properly about themselves and the planet on which they live, so that they can fulfill their lives physically, mentally and spiritually. Fortunately, schools and teachers in America, Russia, China, India, Europe and elsewhere can provide a fine education when they set priorities and make the effort to do so.

In the ancient societies of China, India and Greece schools were established. However, for thousands of years people in nearly all countries, except for the ruling elite, did not attend and were uneducated. The Renaissance was a turning point in the ideas and aims of education. But not until the late 1800s and 1900s were universal elementary systems effectively established in America, Europe, Russia and other countries.[61] However, full literacy hasn't been achieved.

Good schooling is the key to the development of our most valuable asset, our human resources. It is through education that age old prejudice gives way to reason and the scientific spirit. By learning society is modernized and the mind trained. Good schooling erodes narrow barriers and broadens one's vision. Through public education technology is put into the service of the betterment of the individual and the nation.[62]

Choices must be made on how much to spend on education, what to target and how communities can share the responsibility with central governments. But long term decisions have to be made. A week long United Nations Education Conference chaired by the Secretary-General via satellite and two way TV with the leaders of all countries can arrange a historic education agenda and timetable for the coming decade.

Overall literacy on our planet with the guidance of the US President, the Russian President and the United Nations can improve within months. National school systems can be strengthened to bring high quality education to all members of society. Billions of dollars from the military can be directed into education programs.

The United States, Russia and Europe can truly lead the way for the world. A sharp yearly drop in illiteracy will follow. The basic courses, reading, writing and arithmetic can be streamlined in developing and industrial nations. High school can be tailored to meet the needs of individual students. Programs for the exceptionally talented, athletes, artists, the learning disabled and handicapped already used in many schools can be expanded locally. Universities particularly in Africa, Asia and South America will be bustling with bright and energetic students.

Teachers and administrators will be responsible for performance. Those who turn out well educated students should be paid accordingly. Vocational training will be crucial. For those not headed toward college, business, industry and research may provide internships that give students practical experience in the working world they are about to enter.[63]

Without additional capital investment, by rescheduling the hours, education can be expanded dramatically in all countries. The school day and year can be lengthened. Japan's school year consists of 240 eight hour days. America's averages 180 days of about 6.5 hours. The class size can be cut from nearly 18 to 10 students.[64] Volunteer parents, retired people and advanced students can act as tutors. Many big city public school systems will find it necessary to remain open 24 hours a day, retraining adults from 4 pm to midnight and renting out the costly computer and communications systems to local businesses during the late hours.[65]

Students should be promoted based on work and tests and not solely on time in class. Foreign languages need to be emphasized and the study of different cultures to understand traditions. Parents have to take an active interest. Higher academic standards must be set.[66]

The computer revolution going on now is changing dramatically school curriculums at all grade levels. Students in the US, Europe and Japan are gaining greater access and exposure to computers at a younger age. In Russia and Eastern Europe, along with China and India computers are just beginning to be used. However, massive numbers of teachers can be trained and populations educated via telecommunication. In a short period of time in most nations television sets with satellite dishes can be installed in remote villages and learning at all grades will expand. The utilization of technology will greatly accelerate universal education.

In the modern classroom the desktop computer will become popular and widespread. On the screen students will beable to tune into museums, libraries and great universities. Art students will roam the national galleries and view art treasures. Electronic chalkboards for physical education classes can analyze the motion of a play frame by frame. Biology courses will include live pictures. Music videos will allow students to exercise their creativity composing and editing video tape. Historic events will be seen in laserdisc movies. Students will benefit from a wealth of video about life on our beautiful planet.[67]

By the early 21st century most libraries will provide online and network access to local and national data. Media centers will become the gateway to worldwide information.[68] Learning will be a lifelong adventure. People will take nature trips, travel and be part of international yearly exchange programs living in different countries. In the years to come the flowering of education, culture and religion will far surpass the first Renaissance in the 1300s, 1400s and 1500s.

Today, it is both desirable and practical for the US, Russia, Europe and all other governments to halt the fragile condition of housing and education, initiate the necessary changes and in so doing transform civilization.

EPILOGUE

Under the threat of nuclear and environmental annihilation to God's creatures, the spirit of global cooperation has come of age. The post World War II technological breakthroughs and mass media have changed our view of time, space and reality. The boundaries that separate one nation from another are merely convenient demarcations of culture. We are one small planet. For the first time this century the rise of planetary problems are producing a new consciousness, as profound as the city-state 2,500 years ago, the Renaissance in the 1500s, the industrial revolution in the 1800s and Democracy in the 1900s.

Today, six global crisis in weapons, pollution, population, food, energy and housing are converging with terrible consequences for everyone. In the next 24 hours 2 atomic bombs in the US and Russia/CIS will be produced[1] and 3 billion dollars squandered on the military.[2] Deforestation will destroy more than 100,000 acres of tropical forests, and kill 100 species of animals, birds, fish and plants.[3] Sickness and deaths due to acid rain, carcinogens and smog will increase. 250,000 new babies will be born[4] but due to malnutrition, disease and infant mortality many will die. 40,000 people will starve to death.[5] Billions of all ages are in dire need of housing.

GLOBAL RENAISSANCE

There is virtually unanimous agreement that something comprehensive and long term has to be done. The end of the Cold War makes it possible for the kind of changes in national strategies unthinkable at any other point. Polls show that growing numbers of people want their countries to respond.

We are on the threshold of the best and brightest of times. Those entrusted with the powers of government must make decisions for the common good or new leaders will. Given the belief that national survival is at stake conditions considered politically or economically impossible can be accomplished in a remarkably brief time.

World War II mobilized countries all over the planet. Work patterns for men and women were dramatically changed. National goals were set. Resources were redirected and factories retooled. Societies were completely reorganized. After five years the results were a great victory. In the late 1940s the Marshal Plan lead by the United States helped to reconstruct Europe. This comprehensive economic, political, social and cultural program did establish a precedent for massive investment in nations.

The astonishing events in Russia, the commonwealth and Eastern Europe by millions of people in nonviolent revolutions show that unprecedented changes can happen in a matter of months or even a few days. However, after the euphoria and multi-party elections countries need sweeping economic, environmental and energy programs. Prudent policies by all those in charge, especially the superpowers, will avoid groping for direction, chaos and bloodshed.

In the weeks ahead new governments will be elected in Europe, Central America, Asia and Africa which can make a big break with the past. This is a significant situation with unique possibilities. Around the globe peoples actions by getting involved in issues and voting, as well as

EPILOGUE

eating healthy, not polluting and recycling will determine whether the next century will be a golden age or the last one for humankind.

So much that was inconceivable a year ago and unlikely a few months ago has somehow, against all odds, come to pass. With the peace dividends from disarmament and keying in on United Nations standards peoples lives will improve dramatically year after year. By setting a five year time schedule and adhering to it real solutions will result. Without weapons and by solving the underlying problems a safer world will naturally come about.

A healthy environment, modern electronic homes, solar automobiles and a prosperous global economy will develop. As robots spread to more factories and farms are more mechanized, work in all occupations will diminish significantly. People, especially in America and Europe, will have more time to learn and will retire younger. Unprecedented advances in university research worldwide particularly in biomedicine and genetic engineering will see artificial human organ transplants, ways to regenerate damaged nerve tissue, the eradication of Cancer and human life extended to nearly one hundred years.

Survival depends upon everyone doing their part and particularly upon the American President and the Russian President's actions. By the same token, it is through their neglect and others that the planet continues to wither and die. In the event that the US and Russia allow the nuclear weapons and other crisis to go on, such errors will be tantamount to a universal catastrophe. We are at a critical hour in human history. Those in charge must demonstrate their concern for the life and health of people and the planet not in words, but in deeds.

The superpower presidents must act together. The situation does not allow them to wait for the perfect moment. Time is running out. The stewardship of the Earth is in their hands. There are enlightened steps to rid us of these truly terrible problems. The two leaders have the extraordinary power to end the nuclear nightmare, disband, provide global solutions, be statesmen and in so doing transform world civilization. Society is ready for change. People are yearning for it.

When the US President initiates the reforms, and Congress and the multinationals go along, the turning point will be within days. If the major corporations resist and do not see the future in terms of survival, then the delay might go on for awhile. But eventually, global approaches will be adopted. When the Russian President convinces the Parliament and the generals, then the changes will begin immediately. All nations will in turn follow.

Understandably, the military industry complex, built up over decades, might not be easy to dismantle at once. However, we have approached the time where dismantle it must. But in the end one thing is clear, if we are to survive the six global problems have to be solved.

Now it is up to people. We must take charge of our own destiny and decide how we want to live our lives. We are the way for the transformation of the planet and lasting peace. During the next five years the United States, Russia, Europe, China, India, Japan and all countries can divert trillions of dollars from the military and bring on a city, national and Global Renaissance. Where music, the arts, literature, sports, science and individual pursuits come to life. The future promises to be brilliant, where society truly flowers—grand, majestic and mystical.

REFERENCES

INTRODUCTION

1. Department of International Economic and Social Affairs, "Population and Vital Statistics Report," United Nations, New York, 1991, p. 1.
2. Ruth Leger Sivard, "World Military and Social Expenditures 1991," World Priorities Publications, Washington, D.C., p. 16.
3. Ruth Leger Sivard, "World Military and Social Expenditures 1985-86," World Priorities Publications, Washington D.C., p. 5.
4. Department of International Economic and Social Affairs, "Population and Vital Statistics Report," United Nations, New York, 1991, p. 1.
5. World Food Council, "Hunger and Malnutrition in the World," United Nations, New York, 1991, p. 5.
6. Stockholm International Peace Research Institute Yearbook, "World Armaments and Disarmament," Oxford University Press, 1991, p. 16, 18.
7. U.S. Arms Control and Disarmament Agency, "World Military Expenditures and Arms transfers 1990," Washington, D.C., 1991, p.1.
8. United Nations Environment Programme, "The State of the World Environment," Nairobi, 1991, p. 4.

CHAPTER 1
THE FUTURE OF WAR OR PEACE

1. U.S. Department of Energy, "Nuclear Weapons Complex Reconfiguration

Study," 1991, p. 10-11. Department of Energy, "Staffing Budget Module Report," 1991, p.23./Contractors Statistics, Office of Industrial Relations, "Contractor Employment Summary Report," 1991, Washington, D.C., all pages.

2. "The Soviet Weapons Industry; An Overview," Central Intelligence Agency, Washington, D.C., 1986, p. 1.

3. U.S. Department of Defense, "Soviet Military Power 1991," Washington, D.C., p. 39.

4. Encyclopedia Americana, V-14, Grolier Inc., Danbury, Connecticut 1991, p. 222.

5. Ruth Leger Sivard, "World Military and Social Expenditures 1987-88," World Priorities Publications, Washington, D.C., 1988, p. 14.

6. US Arms Control and Disarmament Agency, "World Military Expenditures and Arms Transfer 1990," Washington D.C., 1991, p. 1.

7. C. Weeramantry, "Nuclear Weapons and Scientific Responsibility", Longwood Academic, Wolfeboro, NH, 1987, p. iv.

8. Bruce Berkowitz, "American Security Dilemma's for a Modern Democracy," Yale University Press, New Haven, Connecticut, 1986, p. 109.

9. C. Weeramantry, "Nuclear Weapons and Scientific Responsibility", Longwood Academic, Wolfeboro, NH, 1987, p. 53

10. Ibid, p. 53-54.

11. Ibid, p. 56, 184

12. Department for Disarmament Affairs, "Disarmament Facts: Climatic and Other Global Effects of Nuclear War", UN, New York, 1989, p. 2,3.

13. Alva Stewart, "Chemical Weapons-Their Use and Development," Vance Bibliographies, Monticello, Illinois, 1988, p. 2,4.

14. Ibid, p. 2,3.

15. Ibid, p. 1.

16. U.S. Department of State, "Conference on Chemical Weapons Use 1988," Washington, D.C., 1989, p.2.

17. Boris Krasulin, "Disarmament an Ideal of Socialism," Novosti Press Agency Publishing House, Moscow, 1986, p. 20.

18. US Arms Control and Disarmament Agency, "World Military Expenditures and Arms Transfer 1990," Washington D.C., 1991, p. 3

19. Ibid, p. 10.

20. Ruth Leger Sivard, "World Military and Social Expenditures 1987-88," World Priorities Publishing, Washington, D.C., 1988, p. 9.

REFERENCES

21. The International Institute for Strategic Studies, "The Military Balance 1990-1991," London, p. 217, 223, 216, 221.

22. "Defense & Foreign Affairs Handbook 1990-91," International Media Corporation, Alexandria, p. 1016, 1074.

23. Department for Disarmament Affairs, "Disarmament Facts:Climatic and Other Global Effects of Nuclear War," UN, New York, 1989 p. 13.

24. Ruth Leger Sivard, "World Military and Social Expenditures 1982," World Priorities Publications, Washington, D.C., 1983, p. 19.

25. Ruth Leger Sivard, "World Military and Social Expenditures 1987-88," World Priorities Publications, Washington, D.C., 1988, p.5.

26. Ibid, p.35.

27. Michael Renner, "Wrong Turns," World Watch, September October 1989, Washington, D.C., p. 10.

28. Ruth Leger Sivard, "World Military and Social Expenditures 1989," World Priorities Publications, Washington, D.C., 1989, p. 8.

29. Ruth Leger Sivard, "World Military and Social Expenditures 1987-88, "World Priorities Publications, Washington, D.C., 1988, p. 43,46.

30. US Arms Control and Disarmament Agency, "World Miliary Expenditures and Arms Transfers 1990," Washington D.C., 1991, p. 1.

31. The International Institute for Strategic Studies, "The Military Balance 1990-1991," London, p. 232-33.

32. Nicholas Sims, "The Diplomacy of Biological Disarmament," Macmillan Press:in association with the London School of Economics and Political Science, London, 1988, p. 270.

33. US Arms Control and Disarmament Agency, "World Military Expenditures and Arms Transfer 1990," Washington, D.C., 1991. p. 4.

34. "Defense & Foreign Affairs Handbook 1990-91," International Media Corporation, Alexandria, 1991, p. 1016, 1074-75.

35. UNEP, "The State of the World Environment 1987, New York, p. 46.

36. A.J.S. Rayl, "Save The Planet - Drugs and War," OMNI, Sept. 1989, p. 72.

37. Stockholm International Peace Research Institute, Yearbook 1988, "World Armaments and Disarmament," Oxford University Press, 1988, p. 33.

38. William Eaton, "US Concerned About Shift of Tanks to Siberia," Los Angeles Times, November 16, 1990, p. A13. Marshall Ingwerson, "CFE Pact Signals End to Option of Sudden Soviet Raid On Europe," The Christian Science Monitor, November 19, 1990, p. 2.

39. "David Lauter, "US, Soviets Sign Historic Treaty To Cut Nuclear Arms,"

August 1, 1991, Los Angeles Times, p. A1, A6.

40. "Eliminating Nuclear Weapons," p. 1. Douglas Jehl, "Disarmament," Los Angeles Times, September 28, 1991, p. 10.

41. Serge Schmemann, "Pact Is Exceeded," The New York Times, October 6, 1991, p. 1, p. 11.

42. John Broder, William Tuohy, "NATO to Slash A-Weapons 80%, "October 8, 1991, Los Angeles Times, p. 1.

CHAPTER 2
AIR, LAND AND WATER
TODAY AND TOMORROW

1. United States Environmental Protection Agency, "National Air Pollutant Emission Estimates," Washington, D.C., 1991, p. 2.

2. Organisation for Economic Cooperation and Development, "Environmental Indicators," Paris, 1991, p. 19, 21, 23.

3. U.S. Department of Commerce, "Statistical Abstract of The United States 1990," Washington, D.C., p. 203

4. United Nations Environment Programme, "The State of the World Environment 1991", Nairobi, p. iii.

5. Ruth Leger Sivard, "World Military and Social Expenditures 1991," World Priorities Publishers, Washington, D.C., p. 38.

6. Our Planet, Volume 3, Number 2, "The State of the World Environment 1991," UNEP, Nairobi, p. 12

7. Ruth Leger Sivard, "World Military and Social Expenditures 1991," World Priorities Publications, Washington, D.C., p. 38.

8. United Nations Environment Programme, "The State of the World Environment 1987," Nairobi, p. 9.

9. United Nations Environment Programme, "Annual Report of the Executive Director 1987," Nairobi, 1988, p. 48-49.

10. UNEP, "The State of the World Environment 1987," Nairobi, p. 9.

11. Ibid, p. 16.

12. Council on Environmental Quality, Executive Office of the President, "Environmental Quality 1987-88," Washington, D.C., p. 6.

13. Ibid, p. 16.

REFERENCES

14. Ibid, p. 3.
15. Lester Brown, Christopher Flavin, Edward Wolf, "Earth's Vital Signs," The Futurist, July-August 1988, p. 14.
16. United Nations Fund for Population Activities, "The State of the World Population," 1988, New York, p. 29.
17. United Nations Environment Programme, "The State of the World Environment 1987," Nairobi, p. 19.
18. United Nations Environment Programme, "The State of the World Environment 1991," Nairobi, p. 17, 21.
19. Jim MacNeill, "Strategies for Sustainable Economic Development," Scientific American, September 1989, p. 157.
20. Ibid.
21. Linda Marsa, "Save The Planet - Contaminated Drinking Water," Omni, September 89, p. 46.
22. Ibid
23. Ibid
24. Ibid, p. 108.
25. J.W. Maurits La Riviere, "Threats to the World's Water," Scientific American, September 89, p. 86.
26. U.S. Department of Commerce, "Statistical Abstract of the United States 1990," Washington, D.C., p. 208.
27. United Nations Environment Programme, "Annual Report of the Executive Director 1987," Nairobi, 1988, p. 53-54.
28. U.S. Environmental Protection Agency, "Analysis of Strategies for Protecting the Ozone Layer," prepared for Working Group Meeting, Geneva, 1986, p. 21.
29. United Nations Environment Programme, "The State of the World Environment 1991," Nairobi, p. 11.
30. United Nations Environment Programme, "Annual Report of the Executive Director 1987," Nairobi, 1988, p. 54.
31. United Nations Environment Programme, "The State of the World Environment 1991," Nairobi, p. 13.
32. Central Intelligence Agency, "Handbook of Economic Statistics 1990," Springfield, p. 28.
33. United Nations Fund for Population Activities, "State of the World Population 1988," New York, p. 29.
34. United Nations Environment Programme, "1990 Annual Report of the

Executive Secretary," 1991, Nairobi, p. 1.

35   Executive Office of the President of the United States, "The 21st Annual Report of the Council on Environmental Quality," 1990, Washington, D.C., p 50-51.

36.   U.S. Department of Commerce, "Statistical Abstract of the United States 1990," Washington, D.C., p. 207.

37.   Ruth Leger Sivard, "World Military and Social Expenditures 1989," World Priorities Publishers, Washington, D.C., p. 10.

38.   Robert Frosch, Nicholas Gallopoulos, "Strategies for Manufacturing," Scientific American, September 1989, p. 152.

39.   United Nations Environment Programme, "1990 Annual Report of the Executive Director, 1991, Nairobi, p. 55.

40.   United Nations Environment Programme, "The State of the World Environment," 1991, Nairobi, p. 14.

41.   Council on Environmental Quality, Executive Office of the President, Environmental Quality 1987-88, Washington, D.C., p. 33.

42.   United Nations Environment Programme, "The State of the World Environment," 1991, Nairobi, p.7.

43.   Thomas Graedel, Paul Crutzen, "The Changing Atmosphere," Scientific American, September 89, p. 66-8.

44.   Ibid, p. 48.

45.   Commission of the European Communities, "European File," April 1990, Luxenbourg, p.9.

46.   United Nations Environment Programme, "The State of the World Environment 1987," Nairobi, p. 58.

47.   Ruth Leger Sivard, "World Military and Social Expenditures 1991," World Priorities Publishers, Washington, D.C., p. 34.

48.   United Nations Environment Programme, "The State of the World Environment 1987," Nairobi, p. 51.

49.   Ibid, p. 58.

50.   Cathy Spencer, "Endangered Species and the Future of the Planet," OMNI, January 89, p. 51, 108.

51.   Andrew Revkin, "Cooling Off The Greenhouse," Discover, January 89, p. 30.

52.   Cathy Spencer, "Endangered Species and the Future of the Planet," OMNI, January 89, p. 48.

REFERENCES

CHAPTER 3
POPULATION - PROMISE OR PERIL

1. Nathan Keyfitz, "The Growing Human Population," Scientific American, September 89, p. 119.
2. United Nations Population Fund, "The State of the World Population 1991," New York, p. 42.
3. United Nations Environment Programme, "The State of the World Environment 1987," Nairobi, p. 38.
4. United Nations World Food Council, "The Global State of Hunger and Malnutrition 1988", New York, p. 6.
5. United Nations Environment Programme, "The State of the World Environment 1987," Nairobi, p. 47
6. World Bank, "World Development Report 1988," Washington, D.C., p. 274-5.
7. Nathan Keyfitz, "The Growing Human Population," Scientific American, September 89, p. 120-1.
8. World Bank, "World Development Report 1988," Washington, D.C., p. 274-5.
9. United Nations Environment Programme, "Annual Report of the Executive Director 1987," Nairobi, 1988, p. 4.
10. Nathan Keyfitz, "The Growing Human Population," Scientific American, September 89, p. 120.
11. Central Intelligence Agency, "Handbook of Economic Statistics 1990," Washington, D.C., p. 22-23.
12. United Nations Environment Programme, "The State of the World Environment 1987, Nairobi, p. 21.
13. United Nations World Food Council, "The Global State of Hunger and Malnutrition 1988," New York, p. 2.
14. World Bank, "World Development Report 1988, Washington, D.C., p. 274-5.
15. United Nations Population Fund, "The State of the World Population 1991," New York, p. 25,6,7,1.
16. Ibid, p. 1.
17 United Nations Fund for Population Activities, "The State of World Population 1988, New York, p. 51.

18.   Nathan Keyfitz, "The Growing Human Population," Scientific American, September 89, p. 123.

19.   Ibid, p. 124.

20.   Organisation For Economic Co-operation and Development, "1988 Report, Washington, D.C., p. 35.

21.   Nathan Keyfitz, "The Growing Human Population," Scientific American, September 89, p. 125.

22.   Howard I. Shapiro, "The New Birth Control Book," Prentice Hall Press, New York, 1988, p. 102, 136.

23.   Ibid, p. 78, 199.

24.   Nathan Keyfitz, "The Growing Human Population," Scientific American, September 89, p. 125.

25.   World Health Organization, "Evaluation Of The Strategy For Health For All By The Year 2000," Geneva, 1987, p. 42.

26.   Ibid, p. 8.

27.   Ibid, p. 36.

28.   United Nations Population Fund, "The State of World Population 1991," New York, p. 43-44.

29.   World Health Organization, "Evaluation Of The Strategy For Health For All By The Year 2000, Geneva,1987 p. 70.

30.   Susan Weber, "USA By Numbers," Zero Population Growth, Inc., Washington, D.C., 1988, p. 48.

31.   Organisation For Economic Co-operation and Development, "1988 Report", Washington, D.C., p. 133.

32.   World Health Organization, "Evaluation Of The Strategy For Health For All By The Year 2000," Geneva, 1987, p. 80, 78.

33.   Ibid, p. 72.

34.   Ibid, p. 52.

35.   Organisation For Economic Co-operation and Development, "1988 Report," Washington, D.C., p. 133.

36.   Ibid, p. 135.

37.   Ibid, p. 134.

38.   World Health Organization, "Evaluation Of The Strategy For Health For All By The Year 2000," Geneva, 1987, p. 57.

39.   Organisation For Economic Co-operation and Development, "1988 Report," Washington, D.C., p. 35.

40.   World Health Organization, "Evaluation Of The Strategy For Health For

REFERENCES

All By The Year 2000," Geneva, 1987, p. 10.

41. Donald Henderson, "Smallpox Eradication:A WHO Success Story," World Health Forum, Geneva, 1987, p. 283.

42. World Health Organization, "Evaluation Of The Strategy For Health For All By the Year 2000," Geneva, 1987, p. 80.

43. Ibid, p. 33.

44. Ibid, p. 30, 33.

45. Ibid, p. 37.

46. Ruth Leger Sivard, "World Military and Social Expenditures 1991," World Priorities Publications, Washington, D.C., p. 55.

47. Tamas Fulop, Milton Roemer, "Reviewing Health Manpower Development," World Health Organization, Geneva, 1987, p. 130.

48. World Health Organization, "Evaluation Of The Strategy For Health For All By The Year 2000," Geneva, 1987, p. 52.

49. World Health Organization, "Evaluation Of The Strategy For Health For All By The Year 2000," Geneva, 1987, p. 78.

50. Tamas Fulop, Milton Roemer, "Reviewing Health Manpower Development," World Health Organization, Geneva, 1987, p. 109.

51. World Health Organization, "Evaluation Of The Strategy For Health For All By The Year 2000," Geneva, 1987, p. 30.

52. World Bank, " World Development Report 1991," Washington, D.C., p. 272, 257, 258.

53. World Health Organization, "Evaluation Of The Strategy For Health For All By The Year 2000," Geneva, 1987, p. 46, 42.

54. U.S. Arms Control and Disarmament Agency, "World Military Expenditures and Arms Transfer 1987," Washington, D.C., p. 24.

55. World Health Organiztion, "Evaluation Of The Strategy For Health For All By The Year 2000," Geneva, 1987, p. 70.

56. Ruth Leger Sivard, "World Military and Social Expenditures 1987-88," World Priorities Publishers, Washington, D.C., 1988, p. 43.

CHAPTER 4

FOOD - FEAST OR FAMINE

1. United Nations Fund For Population Activities, "The State of the World Population 1988," New York, p. 33

2.   United Nations Population Fund, "The State of World Population 1991," New York, p. 44.

3.   World Food Council, "Report On The Work Of Its Seventeenth Session," UN, New York, 1991, p. 17.

4.   World Food Council, "Hunger And Malnutrition In The World: Situation And Outlook," UN, New York, 1991, p. 2.

5.   World Health Organization, "Evaluation Of The Strategy For Health For All By the Year 2000," Geneva, 1987, p. 9.

6.   World Food Council, "Hunger And Malnutrition In The World: Situation and Outlook, UN, New York, 1988, p. 4.

7.   World Food Council, "Report On The Work Of Its Seventeenth Session," UN, New York, 1991, p. 5.

8.   World Food Council, "Hunger And Malnutrition In The World: Situation And Outlook," UN, New York, 1991, p. 2.

9.   Pierre Crosson, Norman Rosenberg, "Strategies For Agriculture," Scientific American, September 1989, p. 132.

10.   Cathy Spencer, "An Activists Guide To A Better Earth," Omni, September 1989, p. special section.

11.   Pierre Crosson, Norman Rosenberg, "Strategies For Agriculture," Scientific American, September 1989, p. 128.

12.   Ibid, p. 133.

13.   Ibid.

14.   Ibid, p. 130.

15.   Ibid.

16.   Ibid, p. 132.

17.   Lester Brown, Christopher Flavin, Edward Wolf, "Earth's Vital Signs," The Futurist, July-August 1988, p. 46.

18.   Ibid.

19.   John Robbins, "Diet For A New America," Stillpoint Publishing, 1990, p. 352-53.

20.   Pierre Crosson, Norman Rosenberg, "Strategies For Agriculture," Scientific American, September 1989, p. 132-3.

21.   Council on Environmental Quality, Executive Office of the President, Environmental Quality 1987-88, Washington, D.C., p. 29.

22.   Pierre Crosson, Norman Rosenberg, "Strategies For Agriculture," Scientific American, September 1989, p. 132.

23.   David Kinley, "Organic Farming Gains Ground In The Philippines,"

REFERENCES

World Development, September 1990, UNDP, New York, p. 28.

24. Nikos Alexandratos, "World Agriculture:Toward 2000," Food and Agriculture Organization, New York University Press, 1988, p. 150.

25. Ibid, p. 184.

26. J.W. Maurits La Riviere, "Threats to the World's Water," Scientific American, September 1989, p. 80.

27. Ibid.

28. Ibid.

29. World Bank, "World Development Report 1988," Washington, D.C., p. 149.

30. World Health Organization, "Evaluation Of The Strategy For Health For All By The Year 2000," Geneva, 1987, p. 38.

31. J.W. Maurits La Riviere, "Threats to the World's Water," Scientific American, September 1989, p. 80.

CHAPTER 5

SUN, WIND AND RENEWABLE FUELS

1. U.S. Department of Commerce, "Statistical Abstract of the United States 1990," Washington, D.C., p. 569.

2. U.S. Department of Energy, "Petroleum Supply Annual 1990," Washington, D.C., 1991, p. XV, p. XVIII.

3. Ibid, p. XI, p. XV.

4. U.S. Department of Commerce, "Statistical Abstract of the United States 1990," Washington, D.C., p. 569.

5. Ibid, p. 693.

6. John Gibbons, Peter Blair, Holly Gwin, "Strategies for Energy Use," Scientific American, September 1989, p. 136.

7. United Nations Environment Programme, "The State of the World Environment 1987, Nairobi, p. 58.

8. United States Department of Energy, "Petroleum Supply Annual 1988," Washington, D.C., 1989, p. XI, p. XV.

9. Philip Cruver, "Lighting The 21st Century," The Futurist, January-February 1989, p. 29-30.

10. U.S. Department of Energy, "Petroleum Supply Annual 1990," Washing-

ton, D.C., p. XV-XVI. U.S. Department of Commerce, "Statistical Abstract of the United States 1990," Washington, D.C., p. 695.

11. United States Department of Energy, "International Oil and Gas Exploration and Development Activities 1991," Washington, D.C., p. 53-54.

12. Andrew Revkin, "Tapping the Sea," Discover, July 1989, p. 40.

13. Shawna Vogel, "Wind Power," Discover, May 1989, p. 48.

14. John Gibbons, Peter Blair, Holly Gwin, "Strategies for Energy Use," Scientific American, September 1989, p. 139.

15. Shawna Vogel, "Wind Power," Discover, May 1989, p. 48.

16. Ken Butti, John Perlin, "A Golden Thread-2,500 Years of Solar Architecture and Technology," Van Nostrand Reinhold Company, New York, 1980, p. 29, 32, 37, 68, 74, 109, 200, 228.

17. John Gibbons, Peter Blair, Holly Gwin, "Strategies for Energy Use," Scientific American, September 1989, p. 139.

18. U.S. Department of Commerce, National Oceanic and Atmospheric Administration, "Tide Tables," Washington, D.C., 1991, p. 3.

19. Ginny Carroll, "The Furnace Beneath Us," Newsweek, August 28, 1989, p. 55.

20. William Ruckelshaus, "Toward a Sustainable World," Scientific American, September 1989, p. 170-72.

21. Ruth Leger Sivard, "World Military and Social Expenditures 1991," World Priorities Publications, Washington, D.C., p. 41.

22. Our Planet, Volume 2, Number 3, "The Waste In City Waste," 1990, UNEP, Nairobi, p. 17.

23. Howard Wilson, Paul MacCready, Chester Kyle, "Lessons of Sunraycer," Scientific American, March 1989, p. 90.

24. Larry Wartels, "The Development of Solar Energy In the United States," University of California, Los Angeles, 1985

25. Patrick Lee, "GM Unveils An Advanced Electric Passenger Car," January 4, 1990, Los Angeles Times, Times Mirror, p. D1,6.

26. Gar Smith, "Goodbye Gasbuggy, Hello Maglev," Earth Island Journal, Fall 1990, San Francisco, p.23.

27. "Fell'er Up, Please With Hydrogen," Newsweek Magazine, March 5, 1990, p. 42.

28. United Nations Environment Programme, "The State of the World Environment 1987," Nairobi, p. 45.

29. Solar Energy Research Institute, "Future Cars May Run on Air," The

REFERENCES

Futurist, March-April 1989, p. 5.

30. United Nations Environment Programme, "The State of the World Enviroment 1987," Nairobi, p. 58.

31. U.S. Department of Commerce, "Statistical Abstract of the United States 1990, Washington, D.C., p. 569.

CHAPTER 6
CITIES AND CIVILIATION
IN THE 21ST CENTURY

1.   Homewords, Volume 3, Number 4, Washington, D.C., April 1991, p. 1.
2.   U.S. Department of Commerce, "Statistical Abstract of the United States 1990," Washington, D.C., p. 719.
3.   Department of International Economic and Social Affairs, "Housing and Economic Adjustment," United Nations, New York, 1988, p. 29-30.
4.   Ibid.
5.   United Nations Center For Human Settlement, "The Global Strategy for Shelter to the Year 2000," Nairobi, 1990, p. 3.
6.   United Nations Center for Human Settlement/Habitat, "Global Report on Human Settlements 1987," Nairobi, p. 14-15.
7.   Ibid, p. 77.
8.   Department of International Economic and Social Affairs, "Housing and Economic Adjustment," United Nations, New York, 1988., p. 7.
9.   Ibid, p. 39.
10.   United Nations Center for Human Settlement/Habitat, "Global Report On Human Settlements 1987," Nairobi, p. 77.
11.   "The World Almanac & Book of Facts 1991," World Almanac, New York, p. 773.
12.   United Nations Environment Programme, "The State of the World Environment 1987," Nairobi, p. 97.
13.   U.S. Department of Commerce, "Housing Units Authorized By Building Permits: March 1991," Washington, D.C., p. 3.
14.   Department of International Economic and Social Affairs, "Housing and Economic Adjustment," United Nations, New York, 1988, p. 59.
15.   World Bank, "World Development Report 1988," Washington, D.C., p.

266-7.

16. U.S. Department of Commerce, "Statistical Abstract of the United States 1990," Washington, D.C., p. 719.

17. John Fondersmith, "Down Town 2040", The Futurist, March-April, 1988, p. 9.

18. Ibid, p. 13

19. Bruce Stokes, "The Shrinking House of the Future," Habitats Tomorrow, World Future Society, Bethesda, Md., 1984, p. 30.

20. John Fondersmith, "Downtown 2040," The Futurist, March-April 1988, p. 16, 12, 13.

21. Department of International Economic and Social Affairs, "Housing and Economic Adjustment," United Nations, New York, 1988, p. 31.

22. Ibid, p. 55.

23. Ibid, p. 31.

24. United Nations Center for Human Settlement/Habitat, "Global Report on Human Settlement 1987," Nairobi, p. 37.

25. Ibid, p. 38.

26. U.S. Department of Commerce, Construction Review, July-August 1989, "Markets in China for Building Materials and Supplies," Washington, D.C., p. xiv.

27. Ibid.

28. Ibid.

29. Department of International Economic and Social Affairs, "Housing and Economic Adjustment", United Nations, New York, 1988, p. 18.

30. John Fondersmith, "Down Town 2040", The Futurist, March-April 1989, p. 31.

31. Department of International Economic and Social Affairs, "Housing and Economic Adjustment," United Nations, New York, 1988, p. 19.

32. U.S. Department of Commerce, Construction Review, July-August 1989, Washington, D.C., p. iii, x.

33. Roy Mason, "Architecture 2000," Habitats Tomorrow, World Future Society, Bethesda, Md., 1984, p. 113.

34. U.S. Department of Commerce, Construction Review, July-August 1989, Washington, D.C., p. iii, x.

35. Ibid, x.

36. Department of International Economic and Social Affairs, "Housing and Economic Adjustment," United Nations, New York, p. 48.

REFERENCES

37. Roy Mason, "Architecture 2000," Habitats Tomorrow, World Future Society, Bethesda, Md., 1984, p. 113.

38. Ibid, p. 112.

39. Ibid.

40. Roy Mason, "Underground Architecture," Habitats Tomorrow, World Future Society, Bethesda, Md., 1984, p. 133.

41. Roy Mason, Lane Jennings, "Earth-Sheltered Housing," Habitats Tomorrow, World Future Society, Bethesda, Md., 1984, p. 11.

42. Kirby L. Estes, "The Extra Dimension:Urban Architecture for Tomorrow" Habitats Tomorrow, World Future Society, Bethesda, Md., 1984, p. 127.

43. Roy Mason, "Underground Architecture," Habitats Tomorrow, World Future Society, Bethesda, Md., 1984, p. 134-5.

44. Roy Mason, "Architecture 2000," Habitats Tomorrow, World Future Society, Bethesda, Md., 1984, p. 115-116.

45. Kirby L. Estes, "The Extra Dimension: Urban Architecture for Tomorrow," Habitats Tomorrow, World Future Society, Bethesday, Md., 1984, p. 127.

46. Ibid, p. 128; Roy Mason, "Architecture 2000," Habitats Tomorrow, World Future Society, Bethesda, Md., 1984, p. 116.

47. Michael Renner, "The Transportation Crisis In The Third World," The Futurist, March-April 1989, p. 17.

48. Marcia D. Lowe, "Pedaling into the Future", The Futurist, March-April 1989, p. 18.

49. Jeffrey Kluger, "NASA'S Orbiting Dream House," Discover, May 1989, p. 68-70.

50. World Health Organization, "Evaluation of the Strategy For Health For All by The Year 2000," Geneva, 1987, p. 21-2.

51. World Health Organization, "Bulletin of Regional Health Information 1986-87, New Delhi, 1988, p. 16.

52. Organisation For Economic Co-operation And Development, " 1988 Report," Washington, D.C., p. 135.

53. World Health Organization, "Evaluation of the Strategy For Health For All By the Year 2000, Geneva, 1987, p. 21-2.

54. Marvin Cetron, "Class of 2000," The Futurist, November-December 1988, p. 12.

55. U.S. Department of Education, "Digest of Education Statistics 1990,"

Washington, D.C., p. 10.

56. Marvin Cetron, "Class of 2000," The Futurist, November-December 1988, p. 15.

57. World Health Organization, "Evaluation Of The Strategy For Health For All By The Year 2000," Geneva, 1987, p. 133.

58. Ibid, p. 21-22.

59. Organisation For Economic Co-operation and Development, "1988 Report," Washington, D.C., p. 37.

60. U.S. Arms Control and Disarmament Agency, "World Military Expenditures and Arms Transfer 1987," Washington, D.C., p. 23-24.

61. Encyclopedia Americana, International Edition, Grolier Inc., Danbury Connecticut, 1991, Vol. 9, p. 650-51.

62. Organisation For Economic Co-operation and Development, "1988 Report," Washington, D.C., p. 36.

63. Marvin Cetron, "Class of 2000," The Futurist, November-December 1988, p. 15.

64. Ibid, p. 13.

65. Ibid, p. 10,

66. Ibid, p. 14, 13, 11.

67. John Pellino, "Desktop Video In The Classroom," Media and Methods, September-October 1989, p. 44-5.

68. Ibid, p. 63.

EPILOGUE

1. Ruth Leger Sivard, "World Military and Social Expenditures 1987-88," World Priorities Publications, Washington, D.C., p. 5.

2. U.S. Arms Control and Disarmament Agency, "World Military Expenditures and Arms Transfers 1990," Washington, D.C., 1991, p. 1.

3. United Nations Environment Programme, "The State of the World Environment 1991," Nairobi, p. 17, 21.

4. Department of International Economic And Social Affairs, "Population and Vital Statistics Report," United Nations, New York, 1991, p.1.

5. World Food Council, "Hunger and Malnutrition In The World:Situation And Outlook 1991," United Nations, New York, p. 5.

BIBLIOGRAPHY

INTRODUCTION

Cetron, Marvin, Owen Davies. American Renaissance: Our Life At The Turn Of The 21st Century. New York: St. Martin's Press, 1989.

Cioran, Emile. History and Utopia. New York: Seaver Books, 1987.

Durant, Will. The Renaissance. New York: Simon and Schuster, 1954.

Geiger, Theodore. The Future of the International System: The United States and the World Political Economy. Boston: Allen & Unwin, 1989.

Halbertstam, David. The Next Century. New York: Morrow, 1990

Kidder, Rushmore. Reinventing The Future:Global Goals For The 21st Century. Cambridge, Mass: MIT Press, 1988

Muller, Robert. New Genesis. New York: Doubleday & Company, Inc., 1982.

Mungall, Constance, Digby McLaren, ed., Planet Under Stress: The Challenge of Global Change. New York: Oxford University Press, 1990.

CHAPTER 1
THE FUTURE OF WAR OR PEACE

Adams, Valerie. Chemical Warfare, Chemical Disarmament. Bloomington: Indiana University Press, 1990.

Bobbitt, Philip. Democracy and Deterrence: The History and Future of Nuclear Strategy. New York: St. Martin's Press, l988.

Compliance and The Future of Arms Control:Report of a project sponsored by Center International Security & Arms Control, Stanford University & Global Outlook/Gloria Duffy, project director. Cambridge,Mass: Ballinger, 1988.

Craig, Paul, John Jungerman. Nuclear Arms Race, Technology and Society. New York: McGraw-Hill Book Company, 1990.

Fischer, Dietrich. Winning Peace:Strategies & Ethics for a Nuclear Free World. New York: Crane, Russak, 1989.

Gabraith, James. Balancing Acts - Technology, Finance & The American Future. New York: Basic Books, 1989.

Gray, Colin. War, Peace and Victory: Strategy and Statecraft for the Next Century. New York: Simon and Schuster, 1990.

Lampton, David, Catherine Keyser. China's Global Presence: Economics, Politics and Security. Washington D.C.: American Enterprise Institute for Public Policy Research & The Institute of Southeast Asia Studies, 1988.

Muller, Robert. What War Taught Me About Peace. New York: Doubleday & Company, Inc., 1985.

Rowen, Henry, Charles Wolf, jr., ed.. The Impoverished Superpower. San Francisco: ICS Press, 1989.

Simons, Thomas, jr.. The End of The Cold War. New York: St. Martin's Press, 1990.

CHAPTER 2

AIR, LAND AND WATER

TODAY AND TOMORROW

Abel, P.V. Axiak. Ecotoxicology and the Marine Environment. New York: Ellis Horwood, 1991.

Anzovin, Steven, ed.. Preserving The World Ecology. New York: H.W. Wilson, 1990.

Ausubel, Jesse, Hedy Sladovich. Technology and Environment. Washington, D.C.: National Academy Press, 1989.

Decommissioning of Nuclear Facilities: Feasibility, Needs and Costs. The Organisation for Economic Co-operation and Development: Washington, D.C., 1986.

BIBLIOGRAPHY

Elkington, John, Jonathan Shopley. Cleaning up:U.S. Waste Management Technology and Third World Development. Holmes, Pa: World Resource Institute, 1989.

Hirschhorn, Joel. Prosperity Without Pollution: The Prevention Strategy for Industry and Consumers. New York: Van Nostrand Reinhold, 1991.

Nejat, T., Vezi Roglu, ed..Environmental Problems & Solutions: Greenhouse Effect, Acid Rain, Pollution. New York: Hemisphere Publishers Corp., 1990

Pearce, David, Edward Barbier, Anil Markandya. Sustainable Development:Economics and Environment In The Third World. Elgar Publishing Ltd., 1989

Rifkin, Jeremy. Biosphere Politics:A New Consciousness for a New Century. New York: Crown, 1991.

Schneider, Stephen.H. Global Warming: Are We Entering The Greenhouse Century? San Francisco: Sierra Club Books. 1989.

Severe Accidents in Nuclear Power Plants. The Organisation for Economic Cooperation & Development: Washington,D.C.,1986.

Silver, Cheryl Simon. One Earth, One Future: Our Changing Global Environment. Washington, D.C.: National Academy Press, 1990.

Turner, B.L. The Earth As Transformed By Human Action. London: Cambridge University Press, 1989.

Wilson, E.O, Frances M. Peter. Biodiversity. Washington, D.C.: National Academy Press, 1988.

World Commission on Environment and Development. Our Common Future. London: Oxford University Press, 1987.

United States Congress, House Committee on Science, Space & Technology. Subcommittee on Natural Resources, Agricultural Research & Environment. Environmental Health In The 21st Century. Washington, D.C., 1988.

CHAPTER 3

POPULATION - PROMISE OR PERIL

Berger, Peter, L. A Future South America: Visions, Strategies and Realities. 1988.

Boserup, Ester. Economic & Demographic Relationship In Development. Baltimore: John Hopkins University Press, 1990.

Community Action for Family Planning. The Organisation for Economic Co-operation and Development:Washington, D.C., 1988.

Ha Doan, Bui Dang. The Future of Health and Health Care Systems in the Industrialized Societies. New York: Praeger, 1988.

Institute of Medicine, United States. The Future of Public Health. Washington, D.C.: National Academy Press, 1988.

Onwuka, Ralph,I., Olajide Aluko. The Future of Africa and The New International Economic Order. London:Macmillan, 1986.

Tolba, Mostafa, Asit Biswas, ed.. Earth And Us: Population, Resources, Environment, Development. Boston: Butterworth Heineman, 1991.

Wright, Marcia,Zena Stein, Jean Scandlyn. The Health of Women and Children and the Future of Progressive Health Care in Southern Africa. New York: Columbia University, 1988.

CHAPTER 4
FOOD - FEAST OR FAMINE

Braun, Linda. Spirulina:Food For The Future. Beltsville, Maryland: Aquaculture Information Center, 1988.

Brown, Lester,R. State Of The World 1991. New York: Norton & Company. 1991.

Jacobson, Michael. Safe Food:Eating Wisely In A Risky World. Los Angeles: Living Planet Press, 1991.

Johl, S.S. Future Agriculture in Punjab. Chandigarh, India: Center for Research in Rural and Industrial Development, 1988.

Kutzner, Patricia. World Hunger:A Reference Handbook. Santa Barbara: ABC CLIO, 1991.

Paarlberg, Don. Toward A Well-Fed World. Ames: Iowa State University Press, 1988.

Paddock, Joe, Nancy Paddock, Carol Bly. Soil and Survival: Land Stewardship and The Future of American Agriculture. San Francisco: Sierra Club Books, 1986.

Schwartz, F., ed.. Soy Protein and National Food Policy. Boulder: Westview Press, 1988.

Strong, Maurice. Africa Beyond The Famine: The Case For Hope. Boston: African Studies Center, Boston University, 1989.

BIBLIOGRAPHY

CHAPTER 5
SUN, WIND AND RENEWABLE FUELS

Barkakati, Dispankar. Energy Scene In India: Problems & Prospects. New Delhi: Associated Chambers of Commerce & Industry, 1990.

Bleedorn, Berenice. Creative Leadership For A Global Future. New York: Lang, 1988.

Energy Issues And Options For Developing Countries. New York: Published for the UN by Taylor & Francis, 1989.

Energy 2000: A global Strategy for Sustainable Development: A Report for the World Commission on Environment and Development. Atlantic Highlands, N.J.: Zed Books, 1987.

Goldemberg, Jose. Energy For A Sustainable World. New York: Wiley & Sons, 1988.

Lee, Thomas, Ben Ball, jr., Richard Tabors. Energy Aftermath. Boston: Harvard Business School Press, 1990.

Ogden, J.M., R.H. Williams. Solar Hydrogen-Moving Beyond Fossil Fuels. Washington: World Resources Institute,1989.

Wionczek, Miguel, Oscar Guzman, Roberto Gutierrez. Energy Policy in Mexico: Problems and Prospects for the Future. Boulder, Colorado: Westview Press, 1988.

CHAPTER 6
CITIES AND CIVILIZATION
IN THE 21ST CENTURY

Amis, Philip, Peter Lloyd, ed.. Housing Africa's Urban Poor. New York: St. Martin's Press, 1990.

Apgar, William C. The Nation's Housing: A Review Of Past Trends and Future Prospects for Housing In America. Cambridge, Mass: MIT, 1988.

Bezold, Clement, Rick J. Carlson, Jonathan C. Peckit. The Future of Work and Health. Dover, Mass: Auburn House Publishing, Co., 1987

Johnston, William B., Arnold E. Packer. Workforce 2000: Work and Workers For The 21st Century. Indianapolis: Hudson Institute, 1987.

Kerrigan, William, Gordon Braden. The Idea of the Renaissance. Baltimore: John

Hopkins University Press, 1989.

Stewart, Hugh B. Recollecting The Future: A View of Business, Technology and Innovation in the Next 30 Years. Homewood, IL: Dow-Jones, Irwin, 1989.

Zuboff, Shoshana. In The Age of The Smart Machine. The Future of Work and Power. New York: Basic Books. 1988.

Struyk, Raymond, Margery Turner, Makiko Ueno. Future US Housing Policy:Meeting The Demographic Challenge. Washington, D.C.: Urban Instiute Press, 1988.

Yelling, J.A. Slums and Slum Clearance In Victorian London. Boston: Allen & Unwin, 1986.

World Resources 1990-91: An Assessment Of The Resource Base That Supports The Global Economy. World Resources Institute/International Institute For Environment and Development. New York: Basic Books, 1990.

EPILOGUE

Brzezinski, Zbigniew. The Grand Failure, The Birth and Death of Communism in the Twentieth Century. New York: Scribner, 1989.

Davis, J.C. Utopia and The Ideal Society. Cambridge, England: Cambridge University Press, 1981.

Ferencz, Benjamin, Ken Keyes, Jr. Planethood. Coos Bay: Loveline Books, 1991.

Gorbachev, Mikhail. Perestroika, New Thinking For Our Country and The World. New York: Harper & Row, 1986.

Moving Towards The Year 2000: Global Problems and The Future. Moscow: "Social Sciences Today", Editorial Board, 1987.

McKnight, Stephen A. The Renaissance Origins Of Modernity. Baton Rouge: LSU Press, 1989.

Pattison, Joseph. Acquiring The Future:America's Survival and Success In The Global Economy. Homewood, Il.: Dow-Jones, Irwin, 1990.

Weiner, Jonathan. The Next One Hundred Years: Shaping The Fate Of Our Living Planet. New York: Bantam Books, 1990.

ORGANIZATIONS

What we do as individuals affects the planet and the future. The choices we make in our daily lives have an enormous influence, not only on our health but also on the lives of others.

By making small, but real decisions about the things we do, the food we eat, to recycle, not pollute or to get involved, we can make a better world. By acting locally and thinking globally we can help to insure an extraordinary future.

For those who want to learn more or become involved in issues names, addresses and telephone numbers are listed for organizations.

PEACE

Beyond War Foundation
222 High Street
Palo Alto, CA 94301
415-328-7754

Buddhist Peace Fellowship
 P.O.Box 4650
Berkeley, CA 94704
415-525-8596

GLOBAL RENAISSANCE

Campaign for Peace
and Democracy
P.O. Box 1640
New York, NY 10025-1560
212-724-1157

Catholic Peace Fellowship
339 Lafayette Street
New York, NY 10012

Children the Peacemakers
950 Battery Street
San Francisco, CA 94111
415-981-0916

Clergy and Laity Concerned
198 Broadway, Suite 302
New York, NY 10038
212-964-6730

Friends World Committee for
Consultation
1506 Race Street
Philadelphia, PA 19102
215-241-7250

International Association
Educators for World Peace
P.O. Box 3282
Huntsville, AL 35810-0282
205-534-5501

Lawyers Alliance for
Nuclear Arms Control
43 Charles Street, Suite 3
Boston, MA 02114
617-227-0118

National Peace Institute Foundation
110 Maryland Avenue, N.W.
Washington, DC 20002
202-546-9500

Nukewatch
315 W. Gorham Street
Madison, WI 53703
608-256-4146

Pacifica Foundation
3729 Cahuenga Blvd., W
North Hollywood, CA 91604
818-985-8800

Physicians for Social
Responsibility
1000 16th Street,S.W. #810
Washington, DC 20036
202-785-3777

Professional Coalition
for Nuclear Arms Control
1616 P Street, N.W., #320
Washington, DC 20036
202-332-4823

ORGANIZATIONS

Religious Task
Force
85 S. Oxford Street
Brooklyn, NY 11217
718-858-6882

Sane/Freeze: Campaign
for Global Security
1819 H Street, NW
Washington, DC 20006
202-862-9740

Shalom Center
7318 Germantown Avenue
Philadelphia, PA 19119
215-247-9700

Union of Concerned
Scientists
26 Church Street
Cambridge, MA 02238
617-547-5552

United Campuses to Prevent
Nuclear War
1819 H Street, N.W.
Washington, DC 20006
202-862-9740

Women's Action for
Nuclear Disarmament
691 Massachusetts Avenue
Arlington, MA 02174
617-643-6740

ENVIRONMENT

Acid Rain Information
Clearinghouse
33 S. Washington Street
Rochester, NY 14608
716-546-3796

African Wildlife
Foundation
1717 Massachusetts Ave.NW.
Washington, DC 20036
202-265-8394

Alliance for Environmental
Education
2111 Wilson Blvd.Suite 751
Arlington, VA 22201
703-875-8660

American Cetacean
Society
P.O. Box 2639
San Pedro, CA 90731
213-548-6279

GLOBAL RENAISSANCE

Americans for the
Environment
1400 16th Street, N.W.
Washington, DC 20036
202-797-6665

American Forestry
Association
P.O. Box 2000
Washington, DC 20013
202-667-3300

American Rivers
801 Pennsylvania Ave. S.E.
Washington, DC 20003
202-547-6900

American Society for
Environmental History
323 Martin Luther King
Newark, NJ 07012
201-596-3334

Children of the Green
Earth
P.O. Box 95219
Seattle, WA 98145
206-781-0852

Citizens Clearinghouse for
Hazardous Waste
P.O. Box 3541
Arlington, VA 22216
703-276-7070

Clean Water Action
Project
317 Pennsylvania Avenue,SE
Washington, DC 20003
202-547-1196

Climate Institute
316 Pennsylvania Ave., SE
Washington, DC 20003
202-547-0104

The Coastal Society
5410 Grosvenor Lane, #110
Bethesda, MD 20814
301-897-8616

Conservation Foundation
1250 24th Street, N.W.
Washington, DC 20037
202-293-4800

ORGANIZATIONS

Consumer Pesticide Project
425 Mississippi Street
San Francisco, CA 94105
415-826-6314

Council on Economic Priorities
30 Irving Place
New York, NY 10003
202-420-1133

Cousteau Society
930 W. 21st Street
Norfolk, VA 23517
804-627-1144

Defenders of Wildlife
1244 19th Street, N.W.
Washington, DC 20036
202-659-9510

Earth Island Institute
300 Broadway, Suite 28
San Francisco, CA 94133
415-788-3666

Environmental Action
1525 New Hampshire Ave, NW
Washington, DC 20036
202-745-4870

Environmental Defense Fund
257 Park Avenue South
New York, NY 10010
212-505-2100

Environmental Law
Institute
1616 P Street, NW, #200
Washington, DC 20036
202-328-5150

The Forest Trust
P.O. Box 9238
Santa Fe, NM 87504
505-983-8992

Freshwater Foundation
2500 Shadywood Rd.
Navarre, MN 55392
612-471-8407

Friends of the Earth
530 7th Street, S.E.
Washington, DC 20003
202-544-2600

Greenhouse Crisis Foundation
1130 17th Street, NW, #630
Washington, DC 20036
202-466-2823

GLOBAL RENAISSANCE

Greenpeace
1436 U Street, N.W.
Washington, DC 20009
202-462-1177

International Oceanographic
Foundation
4600 Rickenbacker Causeway
Miami, FL 33149
305-361-4888

National Audubon
Society
950 Third Avenue
New York, NY 10022
212-832-3200

National Clean Air
Coalition
530 7th Street, S.E.
Washington, DC 20003
202-543-8200

National Coalition Against
the Misuse of Pesticides
530 7th Street
Washington, DC 20003
202-543-5450

National Parks and
Conservation Association
1015 31st Street, N.W.
Washington, DC 20007
202-944-8530

National Recycling
Coalition
1101 30th Street, NW, #305
Washington, DC 20006
202-625-6406

National Resources Defense
Council
40 W. 20th Street
New York, NY 10011
212-727-2700

National Toxics Campaign
37 Temple Place, 4th Floor
Boston, MA 021111
617-482-1477

National Wildlife
Federation
1400 16th Street, N.W.
Washington, DC 20036
202-797-6800

ORGANIZATIONS

The Nature Conservancy
1815 N. Lynn Street
Arlington, VA 22209
703-841-5300

Nuclear Waste Project
218 D Street, S.E.
Washington, DC 20003
202-544-2600

Pacific Whale Foundation
101 N. Kihei Rd., Suite 21
Kihei, Maui, HI 96753
808-879-8811

Rachel Carson Council
8940 Jones Mill Rd.
Chevy Chase, MD 20815
301-652-1877

Rainforest Action Network
300 Broadway, Suite 28
San Francisco, CA 94133
415-398-2732

Sierra Club
730 Polk Street
San Francisco, CA 94109
415-776-2211

Soil and Water
Conservation Society
7515 NE Ankeny Rd.
Ankeny, IA 50021
515-289-2331

Student Conservation
Association
P.O. Box 550
Charlestown, NH 03603
603-826-4301

Student Pugwash
1638 R. Street, NW, #32
Washington, DC 20009
202-328-6555

Trust for Public Land
116 New Montgomery Street
San Francisco, CA 9 4105
415-495-4014

US Public Interest
Research Group
215 Pennsylvania Ave., SE
Washington, DC 20003
202-546-9707

Worldwide
1250 24th Street, N.W.
Washington, DC 20037
202-331-9836

GLOBAL RENAISSANCE

World Wildlife Fund
1250 24th Street, NW
Washington, DC 20037
202-293-4800

The Xerces Society
10 SW Ash Street
Portland, OR 97204
503-222-2788

POPULATION

Center for Development
and Population Activities
1717 Massachusetts Ave, NW
Washington, DC 20036
202-667-1142

Population Council
One Dag Hammarskjold Plaza
New York, NY 10017
212-644-1300

Center for Population Options
1012 14th Street, NW #1200
Washington, DC 20005
202-347-5700

Population Crisis Committee
1120 19th Street, NW, #550
Washington, DC 20036
202-659-1833

Global Committee
of Parliamentarians
Population and Development
304 E. 45th Street, 12 Fl.
New York, NY 10017
212-953-7947

Population-Environment Balance
1325 G Street, N.W. Suite 1003
Washington, D.C.
202-879-3000

Planned Parenthood Federation
810 Seventh Avenue
New York, NY 10019
212-541-7800

Population Institute
110 Maryland Avenue, N.W.
Suite 207
Washington, DC 20002
202-544-3300

ORGANIZATIONS

FOOD

American Friends Service
Committee
1501 Cherry Street
Philadelphia, PA 19102
215-241-7000

American Vegan Society
501 Old Harding Highway
Malaga, NJ 08328
609-694-2887

Bread For The World
802 Rhode Island Ave., NE
Washington, DC 20018
202-269-0200

Center for Science
in the Public Interest
1501 16th Street, N.W.
Washington, DC 20036
202-332-9110

Earth Save
P.O. Box 949
Felton, CA 95018
408-423-4069

Food First
1885 Mission Street
San Francisco, CA 94103
415-864-8555

Grassroots International
21 Erie Street
Cambridge, MA 02139
617-497-9180

Hydroponic Society of America
P.O. Box 6067
Concord, CA 94524
415-682-4193

International Alliance
Sustainable Agriculture
1701 University Ave., S.E.
Minneapolis, MN 55414
612-331-1099

Pesticides Action Network
P.O. Box 610
San Francisco, CA 94101
415-541-9140

GLOBAL RENAISSANCE

Public Voice for Food
and Health Policy
1001 Connecticut Ave., NW
Washington, DC 20036
202-659-5930

Natural Organic Farmers
Association
63 Hanover Street
Yalesville, CT 06492
203-269-9391

North American Vegetarian
Society
P.O. Box 72
Doldeville, NY 13329
518-568-7970

Organic Crop Improvement
Association
3185 Township Rd., 179
Bellefontaine, OH 43311
513-592-4983

Oxfam America
115 Broadway
Boston, MA 02116
617-482-1211

World Aquaculture Society
16 E. Fraternity
Louisiana State University
Baton Rouge, LA 70803
504-388-3137

World Hunger Program
130 Hope Street
Providence, RD 02912
401-863-2700

Unitarian Universalist
Service Committee
78 Beacon Street
Boston, MA 02108
617-742-2120

ENERGY

Alliance To Save Energy
1725 K St. NW, Suite 206
Washington, DC 20006
202-857-0666

Alternative Sources of
Energy
107 S. Central Avenue
Milaca, MN 56353
612-983-6892

ORGANIZATIONS

American Council for an
Energy Efficient Economy
1001 Connecticut Ave NW
Washington, DC 20036
202-429-8873

American Solar Energy
Society
 2400 Central Avenue, #B-1
Boulder, CO 80301
303-443-3130

American Wind Energy
Association
1730 N. Lynn Street, #610
Arlington, VA 22209
703-276-8334

Biomass Energy Research
Association
1825 K Street, NW, #503
Washington, DC 20006
202-785-2856

Conservation and Renewable
Energy Referral Service
P.O. Box 8900
Silver Spring, MD 20907
800-523-2929

Edison Electric Institute
1111 19th Street, N.W.
Washington, DC 20036
202-778-6400

Energy Research Institute
6850 Hammock Rd.
Naples, FL 33962
813-793-1922

Environmental and Energy
Study Institute
122 C Street, NW, #700
Washington, DC 20001
202-628-1400

International Association
for Hydrogen Energy
P.O. Box 248266
Coral Gables, FL 33124
305-284-4666

National Electrical
 Manufacturers Association
2101 L Street, N.W.
Washington, DC 20037
202-457-8400

GLOBAL RENAISSANCE

National Hydropower
Association
1133 21st Street, NW, #500
Washington, DC 20036
202-331-7551

Public Citizen
2000 P Street, N.W.
Washington, DC 20036
202-293-9142

Renew America
1001 Connecticut Ave., NW
Suite 719
Washington, DC 20036
202-466-6880

Solar Energy Industries
Association
1730 N. Lynn Street, #610
Arlington, VA 22209
703-524-6100

CITIES & CIVILIZATION

American Association of
Small Cities
Rt. 2, P.O. Box 128
De Leon, TX 76444
817-893-5818

Better World Society
1100 17th Street, NW
Suite 502
Washington, DC 20036
202-331-3770

Center for Community
Change
1000 Wisconsin Ave., NW
Washington, DC 20007
202-342-0519

Center for Urban Policy
Research
P.O. Box 489
Piscataway, NJ 08855-0489
908-932-3133

Common Cause
2030 M Street, NWStudies
Washington, DC 20036
202-833-1200

Countdown 2001
5635 Utah Avenue, N.W.
Washington, DC 20015
202-537-1179

ORGANIZATIONS

Democratic National
Committee
430 S. Capitol Street, SE
Washington, DC 20003
202-863-8000

The Fund for Peace
1755 Mass. Ave., NW #500
Washington, DC 20036
202-797-0882

Global Tomorrow Coalition
1325 G Street, N.W.
Washington, DC 20005
202-628-4016

Institute for Policy
1601 Connecticut Ave., NW
Washington, DC 20009
202-234-9382

Joint Center for
Housing Studies
79 JFK Street
Cambridge, MA 02138
617-495-7908

League of Conservation Voters
320 4th Street, N.E.
Washington, DC 20002
202-785-8683

League of Women Voters
1730 M Street, N.W.
Washington, DC 20036
202-429-1965

Metropolitan Assn Urban
Designers & Environmental
Planners
P.O. Box 722
Church Street Station
New York, NY 10008
914-668-2117

National Center for
Neighborhood Enterprises
1367 Connecticut Ave., NW
Washington, DC 20036
202-331-1103

National Geographic
Society
1145 17th Street, N.W.
Washington, DC 20036
202-857-7000

GLOBAL RENAISSANCE

National League of Cities
1301 Pennsylvania Ave., NW
Washington, DC 20004
202-626-3000

National Urban Coalition
1120 G Street, NW, #900
Washington, DC 20005
202-628-2990

Republican National
Committee
310 1st Street, S.E.
Washington, DC 20003
202-863-8500

Resources for the Future
1616 P Street, N.W.
Washington, DC 20036
202-328-5000

United Nations
42nd St. & 1st Ave.
New York, NY 10017
212-963-1234

Urban Institute
2100 M Street, N.W.
Washington, DC 20037
202-833-7200

Worldwatch Institute
1776 Mass. Ave., NW
Washington, D.C 20036
202-452-1999

World Future Society
4916 St. Elmo Avenue
Bethesda, MD 20814
301-656-8274

AUTHOR

Steven Hackin has been a corporation executive, teacher and writer. He wrote "Voting In America for 200 Years" sponsored by the Democratic and Republican National Committees, NASSP, NAACP and the League of Women Voters, and "Weekend War" an ABC Movie of the Week. He is a graduate of the University of Arizona. For twenty years Steven has been an environmentalist, naturalist and futurist.